VGM Careers for You Series

CAREERS

F O R

INTROVERTS
& Other
Solitary Types

Blythe Camenson

VGM Career Horizons
NTC/Contemporary Publishing Group

Library of Congress Cataloging-in-Publication Data

Camenson, Blythe.
    Careers for introverts & other solitary types / Blythe Camenson.
      p.   cm. — (VGM careers for you series)
      ISBN 0-8442-6385-0 (cloth). — ISBN 0-8442-6386-9 (pbk.)
      1. Vocational guidance—United States. 2. Introversion.
    I. Title. II. Series.
    HF5382.5.U5C2518   1998
    331.7′02′0973—dc21   98–29474
                                              CIP

Published by VGM Career Horizons
A division of NTC/Contemporary Publishing Group, Inc.
4255 West Touhy Avenue, Lincolnwood (Chicago), Illinois 60646-1975 U.S.A.
Copyright © 1999 by NTC/Contemporary Publishing Group, Inc.
Printed in the United States of America
International Standard Book Number: 0-8442-6385-0 (cloth)
                                       0-8442-6386-9 (paper)

18   17   16   15   14   13   12   11   10   9   8   7   6   5   4   3   2   1

Contents

Acknowledgments

The author would like to thank the following professionals for providing information about their careers.

Jim Anderson, Stained Glass Artist

Patricia Baker, Costumer

Susan Broadwater-Chen, Information Specialist

Robyn Carr, Novelist

Nick Delia, Letter Carrier

Tom Gerhardt, Cooper

Jan Goldberg, Freelance Writer

Jim Haskins, Biographer

Deb Mason, Potter

Ronald Miller, Conservation Specialist

Stephen Morrill, On-Line Instructor

Valarie Neiman, Researcher

Carol Perry, Travel Writer

Peggy Peters, Freelance Illustrator

Joel Ponz, Joiner

Rosalind Sedacca, Advertising Copywriter

Timothy J. Speed Jr., Security Supervisor

CHAPTER ONE

Careers for Introverts

Perhaps you consider yourself an introvert—you're shy. Or maybe you just prefer to be independent, allowed to work on your own without having to answer to a boss or deal with a lot of different people. You're more comfortable working with things or ideas than with customers or clients. You're happiest when you're working alone.

Although almost every job out there involves at least some minimal contact with other people, there is a wide range of careers for those of you who prefer to go it solo.

In *Careers for Introverts* you will find a selection of professions with a variety of background and training requirements, but they all have one common thread: they're ideal for the autonomous individualist.

Choosing Your Field

People involved with independent work give of themselves in many different capacities, providing a variety of valuable services. If you're reading this book, chances are you're already considering a career in one of the many areas of this wide-open occupational category.

But perhaps you're not sure of the working conditions the different fields offer or which area would best suit your personality, skills, and lifestyle. There are several factors to consider when deciding which sector to pursue. Each field carries with it different levels of responsibility and commitment. To identify occupations that will match your expectations, you need to know what each job entails.

Ask yourself the following questions and make note of your answers. Then, as you go through the following chapters, compare your requirements to the information provided by the professionals interviewed inside. Their comments will help you pinpoint the fields that interest you and eliminate those that clearly would be the wrong choice.

- How much time are you willing to commit to training? Some skills can be learned on the job or in a year or two of formal training; others can take considerably longer.

- Do you want to work behind a desk in a home office, or would you prefer to be out and about working alone in parks or forests or even delivering the mail?

- Can you handle a certain amount of stress on the job, or would you prefer a self-paced workload?

- How much money do you expect to earn starting out and after you have a few years' experience under your belt? Salaries and earnings vary greatly in each chosen profession.

- How much independence do you require? Do you want to work completely alone, or will you be comfortable with varying degrees of contact with coworkers, supervisors, or clients?

Knowing what your expectations are then comparing them to the realities of the work will help you make informed choices.

Ideal Careers for Introverts

Writers

Writers are well known for working alone. Nothing can stop the creative flow more for a writer than the sound of a phone ringing or another human voice. Full-time writers sit by themselves at their computers for hours a day. And though, just as with artists, they need other people to sell their work, most contacts can be handled through the mail. An agent's phone call to report a sale is the only welcome interruption.

Artists

Perhaps no other endeavor conjures an image of solo workers better than that of talented artists, struggling by themselves in a studio (or garret) with nothing for companionship other than a radio and the smell of linseed oil and paint. While it's true that some artists use models, many others work with props or paint from memory. And though at some point most studio and commercial artists might have to venture out among people to sell their work, most of their time is spent in solitary creation.

Researchers

Would your ideal job allow you to keep your nose in a book or scan the thousands of sites on the Internet? If so, then a freelance research position might be the career for you.

Computer Professionals

Computer professionals have many avenues to pursue and many of these involve working independently. From systems analyst to on-line instructor, there are nearly as many career titles as there are people interested in this field.

Forest Rangers

Picture yourself in a pristine forest, where the only sounds are the wind blowing through the trees, the rustle of leaves as small creatures scamper by. In national parks and forests, rangers are hired to watch for fires and protect against unlawful hunting or logging or any disturbances, human or otherwise, that would upset the balance of nature. Park rangers also work with people to some extent, functioning as guides or interpretative rangers.

Security Guards

Security guards, and most often nighttime security officers, have lonely and sometimes boring jobs. It's not a career for anyone but the introverted type who enjoys quiet and solitude. But introverts working as security guards also have to be prepared for intrusions. After all, they are hired to look out for trespassers, vandals, or other criminals, and though a quiet shift is the ideal, sometimes the work pace is anything but.

Mail Carriers

Each day, the U.S. Postal Service receives, sorts, and delivers millions of letters, bills, advertisements, and packages. To do this, it employs about 792,000 workers. Almost half of these workers are postal clerks, who sort mail and serve customers in post offices, or mail carriers, who deliver the mail.

Although mail carriers spend some time each day at the post office, collecting the mail for their routes and interacting with coworkers and supervisors, much of their time is spent working independently as they deliver the mail.

The Qualifications You'll Need

Because the careers in which independent types can exercise their talents vary so greatly, it is understandable that so will the requirements and qualifications for employment. More and more professional jobs require at least a bachelor's degree. However, there are some professions highlighted here that require applicants to have certain specialized skills rather than diplomas.

This chart lists many of the careers featured in the following pages. Pinpoint the job that interests you, then look to the right to find the education or training requirements. Each job's prerequisites will be covered more fully in the chapters ahead.

Education Requirements

Job Title	HS	B.A./B.S.	M.A./M.S.	Ph.D.	Other
Writers					X
Artists		X^P			X
Researchers		X^P			X
Computer Professionals		X^R			
Security Guards	X				
Forest Rangers		X^R			
Mail Carriers	X				

^{P}=Preferred ^{R}=Required

Salaries

Just as the required qualifications differ, so do salaries. How much you'll earn will depend on your work setting, your employer, your level of education and training, as well as the geographic area in which you live. Throughout the following chapters you will learn more about the specific salaries professionals in each featured career can expect to draw.

For More Information

In the Appendix you will find professional associations for many of the career paths explored in this book. Most offer booklets and pamphlets with career information; some are free, others might have a nominal charge of one or two dollars. A letter will have information in the mail to you within a few days.

CHAPTER TWO

Writers

Although writers come from all sorts of backgrounds and
are different from one person to the next, they do have
a few things in common. For one thing, they are more
than comfortable working alone. In fact, for most writers, solitude
is a necessity.

Writers also share a love of words. They love how the words
sound and how they fit together in original and rhythmic ways.
They love playing with an idea and letting it grow until it
becomes a workable article, advertisement, story, novel, or nonfiction book.

They love seeing the words fill their computer screens and print
in neat lines on what was once a blank sheet of paper. They love
the sense of accomplishment they feel when a project has been
completed, when it satisfies a client or finds a home in a book or
magazine.

They love seeing their names in print, giving them credit for
their writing, and they love receiving the check, which in essence
says "thanks for a job well done."

However, there are frustrations and disappointments, too.
Becoming a professional writer is not an easy task. New writers
face stiff competition from experienced writers with proven track
records. Impersonal rejection slips become a way of life for new
writers, who sometimes must wonder if they have better chances
at winning the lottery than getting published.

But new writers do get published every year (a lot more than
lucky lottery winners). It takes persistence, knowledge of the rules
of the trade, and a little luck, but if it's what you want more than
anything else, you *can* make it happen.

In this chapter we will cover all the different writing careers and how you can get started. You will also meet several successful writers and learn what the writing life is like for them.

Novelists

Fiction writers are creative, imaginative people. After all, they have to be; they make up stories for a living. Whether writing short stories or full-length novels, fiction writers have to be able to create imaginary characters and events and make them seem real to their readers.

Fiction writers have to be troublemakers, too, inventing all sorts of problems for their characters. They have to make their conversations and thoughts entertaining and fill their characters' lives with action. Finally, fiction writers have to be expert problem solvers, helping their heroes find satisfying solutions to their troubles by the end of the story.

If you love to read fiction and you find yourself stopping in the middle of a book and saying out loud, "I could do that better," then maybe you can.

The Novelist's Life

Few new fiction writers have the luxury of working at their craft full-time. Most need to maintain some other sort of employment to help pay the bills until they are able to support themselves through their writing. Because of this, dedicated writers use every spare minute they have to work on their books or stories. John Grisham, for example, wrote a good deal of *The Firm* on yellow legal pads while taking the train to and from work as a full-time attorney in a law firm.

Others get up an hour early, stay up an hour late, turn down invitations to parties or other social events, or let the housework go—whatever they can do to find the time to write.

Successful authors who support themselves through their writing treat it as a full-time job. Most report learning how to discipline themselves to put in a certain number of hours each day.

Every writer chooses a schedule that is comfortable. Some work in the early hours of the morning, take afternoon naps, then go back to the computer in the evenings. Others write for eight or ten or twelve hours straight each day for a period of months until the book is finished. Still others might take years to complete one volume.

There is no set formula for how a writer should work. The only rule is that you have to write. Author James Clavell said that even if you write only one page every day for a year, at the end of that time you'll have 365 pages. And that's a good-size book.

The Many Categories of Fiction

Next time you visit a bookstore, take note of where the different books are shelved and what the signs in each section say. Here is an example of some of the different genres or categories you'll encounter, along with a few of their subgenres.

General/Mainstream	Romance
Action/Adventure	Contemporary
Children's	Historical
Fantasy	Gothic
Historical	Regencies
Horror	Sensuous
Literary	Sweet
Science Fiction	Suspense
Mystery	Psychological
Cozy	Thriller

Crime   Western

Detective   Young Adult

Police Procedural

How to Get Published

Writing a short story or a full-length novel is only half the battle. In addition to honing your skills as an expert storyteller, you also have to be a knowledgeable salesperson. That means you must learn which publishers to approach and how to approach them. Several of the market guides mentioned at the end of this chapter will tell you what categories of fiction the different publishers buy. The guides also list the different magazines that purchase short stories. You can also check your own book collection to learn who publishes books similar to what you want to write.

Once you've made a list of possible markets, you need to make sure your approach is appropriate. Your manuscript needs to be typed and double spaced, with page numbers and your name at the top of each page. Most writing how-to books can give you the information you need to format your manuscript properly.

Before you send in your completed manuscript, you should write the editor a brief query letter describing your project. You can also include a one-page synopsis, or summary, of your book's plot and the first two or three chapters of your book as a sample, if that's the way a particular publisher prefers to be approached. Don't forget to enclose an SASE, a self-addressed, stamped envelope. The editor will use this to send you a reply. If the editor likes your submission, you'll probably receive a request to send more.

Alternatively, you can look for an agent first, following the same steps you'd use to make your initial approach to a publisher. But this time, you are asking that the agent consider you as a possible client.

At this point, after the query letters and sample chapters are in the mail, many new writers just sit back and wait for responses. Smart writers put that manuscript out of their heads and get to work on the next one. And the next one. And the next one.

In the end, the key to getting published can be summed up in one word: persistence.

The Rewards, the Pay, the Perks

"Don't give up your day job just yet." That's what the experts advise. Even if you manage to break in and sell your first novel, you can expect to receive only about $2,500 to $5,000.

The six-figure advances that some superstar authors receive are not the norm. Zebra Books senior editor John Scognamiglio says, "That kind of stuff, like with John Grisham, doesn't really have anything to do with the rest of us. There are 110,000 new titles a year and there are only fifteen on the *New York Times Bestseller List* at a time. Most of the rest of us are going to make a moderate income and do a civilized business if we work very, very hard. There's not that much room at the top. And there isn't much of a middle class in publishing. You either make a little bit of money, which the grand majority will do, or you make a lot."

If you do manage to land that first book contract, you will receive an advance against royalties. A royalty is a percentage, usually 6 to 10 percent, of the money your book earns in sales. The advance is paid half on signing the contract, half on deliverance and acceptance of the manuscript.

But money is not the only reason writers write. For some, the profession is almost an obsession—a burning desire to put words to paper, to start a book and see it to its finish. They wouldn't be happy doing anything else.

Other perks include recognition and publicity, though some might view the attention as a downside. Many writers report that the nicest perk is being able to go to work in a bathrobe.

What It's Really Like

Robyn Carr, Novelist

Robyn Carr has written fourteen books since 1980, most in the historical romance or category romance genre. But recently, she switched genres and her latest book, *Mind Tryst*, is an excellent psychological suspense/thriller published by St. Martin's Press. Robyn also taught for the Writer's Digest School of Writing and is the author of *Practical Tips for Writing Popular Fiction* (Writer's Digest Books).

HOW ROBYN CARR GOT STARTED   "I'm a very ordinary person. I've been married twenty-two years, I have a couple of kids—until recently I even drove a station wagon. While I was pregnant, I read a lot and thought anybody with half a brain could do this, which is how everyone thinks in the beginning. You write that first book and you're sure it's going to be *Gone with the Wind*, but it's really junk. But something happens to you when you're doing it. It held my interest to the point that it became an obsessive desire to write. I couldn't wait to get back to it."

SWITCHING FROM ROMANCE TO SUSPENSE   "I was scared to try at first, and then scared that I wasn't very good at it. I had spent twelve to fourteen years in romance; I had read everything that had been written and I was getting burnt out. It was hard to find anything new. I was tired of writing it and tired of reading it. But I'm not tired of suspense—it's sort of like traveling. I've been through romance, now I'm in psychological suspense, and who knows where I'll go next."

CONSTRUCTING PLOTS   "There are so many things to remember when writing a suspense novel. I pass my manuscript through a couple of readers before I ever send it to my agent, and I get notes in the margins like, 'Are we ever going to find out what happens to this?'

"With romance I just use notes and simple 1, 2, 3, a, b, c outlines. But in suspense so much rests on when certain discoveries are made. I have to make plot outlines on index cards so that I can lay them out on the table and move them around. For example, at what point will Jackie discover things about Tom Wall (lead characters in *Mind Tryst*)? Or when does Jackie use the gun? One of the rules of writing is if you introduce a gun into a story, you'd better use it. At some point during the writing of this book I decided she had to have a gun, and I put that gun on index cards. 'Gun hidden in laundry room closet. Gun kept on the back of the toilet while she showers.' I could put those index cards in certain places in the story and move them around. How these elements are arranged throughout the book is important to the reader."

MISTAKES TO AVOID   "A classic mistake made by new writers, and made by me so many times, is confusing building suspense with withholding information. But it's exactly the opposite. The more information you give, the more suspense you build.

"Another problem with keeping secrets is that it breaks a hard and fast rule. If your main character, from whose viewpoint the story is written, knows something, the reader also has to know it. The information can be kept secret from other characters, but the reader is in her head and the character can't hide her thoughts from the reader.

"The first rule of mystery is that your readers are entitled to an equal opportunity with your characters to solve the mystery."

THE WRITING PROCESS   "I was on a panel at a writer's conference, and someone who wanted to write a book stood up and asked, 'What should you do? Should you force yourself to write the book from beginning to end, should you outline first, should you revise as you go along?' and everyone on the panel of six published authors—and some of them were very successful and making tons and tons of money—said that you should really outline first and force yourself to write through and then revise. However, I keep getting stuck going back to the beginning and revising and revising before I can carry on.

"Before I begin, I have a real clear idea what's going to happen. Some minor things change but the basic premise—who the bad guy is and how it's going to end—is real solid. I can't get past fifty pages without revising twenty times, and then I can't get past one hundred pages without revising twenty times, and when I really hit my stride and the momentum takes me through to the end is at about three hundred pages.

"Until I've written an entire book I'm not clear on what my characters' personalities are and how they feel about things. I'm always too passive in the first draft, reluctant to say someone is so fat Omar the Tentmaker has to make her gown. I'll say that she's overweight or she's a little on the chubby side. Or I give people emotions like, *uncomfortable*—passive stuff—until I can finally get down and dirty about how they really feel. They're either angry or they're not, they're either scared or they're not—but they're not uncomfortable.

"Another problem is the expression 'she felt numb,' or 'she didn't know how she felt.' Which usually means I don't know what she's feeling. But that won't work in fiction. The personality has to be clearly defined."

ROBYN CARR'S FIRST SALE   "My first agent lived in San Antonio. He'd just opened the agency and was trying to build it up. He was my fourth or fifth attempt. I had been submitting things on my own before. I wrote query letters and killed myself hammering out synopses and revising the first three chapters four hundred times. I would get the envelope ready for the next submission before the rejection came so I wouldn't be paralyzed with grief.

"My agent made multiple copies and sent it to thirteen publishers—the thirteenth publisher took it. Avon, Bantam, and Berkley rejected it and my heart was sinking lower and lower. I knew there was no hope, then Little Brown & Company finally bought it and I said, 'Little who?' It is one of the finest publishers in America but I hadn't heard of it.

"My first novel, *Chelynne*, was published in 1980."

Freelance Writers

Although many writers work as staff writers for newspapers and magazines, in the remainder of this chapter we will focus on freelancers who work independently for a variety of clients.

Many freelancers start out working as staff writers until they establish themselves; others set up shop in a home office right away, selling their work to publishers or different kinds of publications, manufacturing firms, and public relations and advertising departments or agencies. They sometimes contract to complete specific assignments, such as writing about a new product or technique. There are many people—business owners or politicians, for example—who hire the services of professional writers to do their writing for them because they lack either the skill or the time.

You can keep busy writing magazine ads, travel brochures, political speeches, or press releases. The possibilities are as varied as the number of clients you can develop.

What the Work Involves

Freelancers could take on a variety of roles as writers. Here are four examples.

1. *Advertising copywriters* write all the words for magazine ads and radio and TV commercials. To describe a business's

services or a client's product, they write the copy for brochures or pamphlets. They write all the copy for direct-mail packages, which are used to sell products or services, such as magazine subscriptions or memberships in a book club, through the mail.

2. *Ghostwriters* write books for people who don't have the necessary skill to do it themselves. The client could be a famous person, such as a former president or a movie star, who has a story to tell but needs help telling it. Ghostwriters sometimes get credit for their writing (you might see "as told to" on the book jacket cover), but many times they remain anonymous, writing behind the scenes.

3. *Press secretaries* work for government officials, actors, or big corporations that are concerned with relations with the press. They schedule public appearances and read prepared statements to reporters. They also write press releases, which are announcements of events, services, or products. Press releases are sent to various newspapers and TV and radio shows in the hope of receiving some free publicity.

4. *Speech writers* work with politicians and other public figures, listening to what they want to say, then writing the speeches they will deliver. When you listen to the president on the television or see the mayor or governor speaking to a group of voters, you can make a good bet that the speech was written by someone else.

Finding Clients

Many writers work for an ad agency, gaining experience and making contacts, before striking out on their own. Others might start with just one client, such as a big corporation that sends enough work their way. Through building a reputation as a good worker who delivers on time, you will receive recommendations from your clients, and that will lead you to new clients. Word of mouth is how most writers build business.

The Rewards, the Pay, the Perks

In many careers, especially in the various areas of the writing profession, you'll hear the expression "the work is its own reward." What that means is the money you make doing that work isn't particularly exciting. But in the case of writing for others, the money can be as rewarding as the work.

Most people who write for others do it on a freelance basis. Although some charge a flat hourly rate, most charge by the project. It can be feast or famine starting out, but once you build a steady client base, your income can be very attractive.

Writers who do earn straight salaries work for magazines, newspapers, advertising agencies, and public relations firms. Salaries can range from less than $20,000 a year for entry-level positions all the way up to $75,000 or more for experienced and successful employees.

Here are some examples of what freelancers charge for a few selected projects. These figures are averages; amounts vary according to the size and scope of the project, the client's industry, and the geographic region.

Sample Freelance Writing Fees

	HOURLY	BY THE PROJECT
Advertising copywriting	$20 to $100	$200 to $4,000
Book jacket copywriting		$100 to $600
Brochures	$20 to $50	$200 to $4,000
Business Catalogs	$25 to $40	$60 to $75 per printed page

Direct-mail packages		$1,500 to $10,000
Encyclopedia articles		$60 to $80 per 1,000 words
Ghostwriting	$25 to $100	$400 to $25,000 or 100% of the advance and 50% of the royalties
Greeting Cards		$20 to $200 per verse
Press Kits		$500 to $3,000
Press Release		$80 to $300
Speech Writing	$20 to $75	$100 to $5,000 (depending upon the client)
Technical Writing	$35 to $75	$5 per page

The Pleasures and Pressures of Freelance Writing

Independence is one of the pluses freelancers will tell you about. For many jobs or projects, you can do your work in a home office, delivering the project when it's finished. You choose the projects you want to work on, and you set your own salary or fees.

The downside is that you have to learn how to promote yourself and seek out clients. In the beginning you might have to call strangers on the phone or knock on office doors looking for work.

When you do have work, you'll also have deadlines. This means you'll have to deliver on time.

And some writers have a hard time asking for money. They would love to leave the business end of things to someone else.

But when you are a freelance writer, you have to wear all the different hats. It's up to you to set the fee, draw up the invoices, and bill the client. It's also up to you to collect from clients if they are late or if it seems they might not pay at all.

What It's Really Like

Rosalind Sedacca, Advertising Copywriter

Rosalind has been writing advertising copy for brochures, magazine ads, and television commercials for more than fifteen years. She feels that it's always important to meet your deadlines and to give your clients a little more than they're asking for. This way they'll always feel they're getting their money's worth.

THE ROLE OF AN ADVERTISING COPYWRITER   "I write ads for magazines, TV and radio commercials, brochures, direct-mail packages, video scripts, newsletters, sales letters, and any other kind of material that needs to be written to help a company sell its product.

"When you write an ad, the first thing you have to know is what the purpose is. Then you want to understand who the market is, who will eventually be reading your writing. You have to understand the demographics—their age, their background, their sex, their income, their education level, and their interests. If I'm writing a print ad for a teenage audience, I'm going to write it a lot differently from an ad for mothers or engineers.

"I work in tandem with other creative people who are graphic designers. I do the writing, and the graphic designers take care of the layout and art. We team up and brainstorm; the words alone don't work unless they're placed on the page in attractive ways.

"The goal is to get people to visit, to buy, to subscribe, or to join. The products I write copy for include computers, hotels and resorts such as Club Med, banks and real estate companies, car and appliance manufacturers, museums, magazines, all sorts of things."

HOW ROSALIND SEDACCA GOT STARTED   "I got started out of college wanting to work for *Vogue* magazine in the editorial department. I thought I wanted to work in the fashion world. I grew up in New York City and I went to the personnel department, but there weren't any openings. Instead, they offered me a position in advertising. I went to work as an assistant to the woman who was writing subscription letters, the ones you receive in the mail offering you subscriptions to different magazines.

"A year later, she left the company and I became creative director of circulation promotion for Condé Nast Publications, which owns *Vogue, Glamour, Mademoiselle, House and Garden*, and *Bride's*. It was a pretty cushy job for someone who was twenty-one years old. It inadvertently made me a direct-mail/advertising expert. I was with Condé Nast for two years, then I left and moved into more general advertising for various advertising agencies in New York City, St. Louis, and Nashville.

"In 1984 I went out on my own, and I've been independent since then."

THE UPSIDES OF FREELANCE WRITING   "It's very stimulating and creative. I never get bored; no two days are ever the same. What I like best, and what also can be a challenge, is that one minute I'm writing about a hotel and the next minute I'm writing about a computer, and then I'm turning around and writing about a bank or about shoes. Sometimes it's hard to change mental gears to focus from one topic to another. It's the plus and the minus together.

"But I've got a perfect mix. Part of the week I'm in my home office working at the computer. I don't have to get dressed, no one sees me, I'm just on the phone a lot. The other part of the week I'm at meetings, either getting new clients or delivering my work, and then I'm dressed to the hilt and showing myself as a professional."

THE DOWNSIDES OF LIFE AS A FREELANCER "The phone can take a lot of my time, and I have to wear many hats. I do my own accounting and taxes, filing—all that administrative work, such as sending bills to clients. I'd much rather be writing, but in a small business you have to do everything.

"And when you start out, the finances can be tricky at first. Feast or famine. But now it's smoothed out for me; I've been in business for a long time."

Writing for Magazines

Visit any bookstore or newsstand and you will see hundreds of magazines covering a variety of topics—from sports and cars to fashion and parenting. There are also many you won't see there, the hundreds of trade journals and magazines written for businesses, industries, and professional workers in virtually every career.

These publications all offer information on diverse subjects to their equally diverse readership. They are filled with articles and profiles, interviews and editorials, letters and advice, as well as pages and pages of advertisements. But without writers, there would be nothing but advertisements between their covers—and even those are produced by writers!

Whether you work for a magazine full-time or as an independent freelancer, you will discover that there is no shortage of markets where you can find work or sell your articles.

The Difference Between Staff Writers and Freelancers

A staff writer is employed full-time by a publication. She or he comes into work every day and is given article assignments to research and write or works with an editor to develop ideas.

A freelance writer works independently, in rented office space or in a home office. Most freelance writers plan and write articles and columns on their own and actively seek out new markets in which to place them.

Staff writers might have less freedom with what they choose to write, but they generally have more job security and always know when the next paycheck will arrive. Freelancers trade job security and regular pay for independence.

Both freelancers and those permanently employed have to produce high-quality work. They have editors to report to and deadlines to meet.

Types of Articles

Articles fall into two broad categories: those that educate and those that entertain. Here is just a small sampling of the topics that magazine articles cover.

Art	Hobbies
Aviation	Humor
Business and Finance	Military
Careers	Nature
Child Care	Pets
Computers	Photography
Contemporary Culture	Politics
Entertainment	Psychology and Self-Help
Food	Retirement
Gardening	Science
General Interest	Sports
Health	Travel

Although the subject matter can be very different, most magazine articles include many of the same elements. They all start with an interesting "hook," that first paragraph that grabs the reader's (and the editor's) attention. They use quotes from real people, mention important facts, and sometimes include amusing anecdotes or experiences.

How to Get That First Article Published

Before starting, read as many magazines as you can, and in particular, those you would like to write for. It's never a good idea to send an article to a magazine you have never seen before. Being familiar with the different magazines will also help you come up with future article ideas.

Once you have decided what you want to write about, there are two ways you can proceed. You can write the entire article "on spec," sending it off to appropriate editors and hoping they like your topic. Or you can write a query letter, a mini-proposal, to see if there is any interest in your idea first. Query letters save you the time of writing articles you might have difficulty selling. Only once you're given a definite assignment do you then proceed. If you are an unpublished writer, editors may tell you to submit the article on spec, meaning that they want to see the whole article, but they won't make a commitment to publish—or pay you for the work—until they see what you can do. There are three important keys to keep in mind to get your articles published:

1. Make sure your writing is polished and that your article includes all the important elements.

2. Make sure your letter and manuscript are neatly typed and free of mistakes.

3. Make sure you are sending your articles to the right publication. A magazine that features stories only on "Planning the Perfect Wedding" will not be interested in your piece on "Ten Tips for the Perfect Divorce."

You can find out about different magazines and the kind of material they prefer to publish in the market guides listed in at the end of this chapter.

The Rewards, the Pay, the Perks

Most writers are thrilled to see their "bylines," that is, their names in print, giving them credit for their writing. And to writers, nothing is more exciting than seeing their stories in print.

Getting a check or a salary for your efforts can be rewarding as well, but sadly, for new freelancers, the checks might not come often enough and are not always large enough to live on.

While staff writers are paid a regular salary (though generally not a very high one), freelancers get paid only when they sell an article. Fees range from as low as $5 to $1,000 or more, depending upon the publication. Even with a high-paying magazine, writers often have to wait until their story is published before they are paid. Because publishers work so far ahead, planning issues six months or more in advance, payment could be delayed from three months to a year or more.

To the freelancers' advantage, sometimes the same article can be sold to more than one magazine or newspaper. These "resales" help to increase salaries. You can also be paid additional money if you provide your own photographs to illustrate your articles.

Getting Started

Freelance writers don't need a long, impressive resume to sell their first article. The writing will speak for itself. If you are sending a query letter, you might want to include "clips," or samples of previously published articles, especially if you have something on a similar topic.

Staff writers sometimes start out as editorial assistants and show their talents while on the job, leading them into a promotion. But to get a full-time, permanent position or regular assignments from a publication, writers must be able to show a successful track record and a portfolio of published clips showcasing their best work.

What It's Really Like

Carol Perry, Travel Writer

Carol Perry has been a travel writer for more than ten years. She also writes novels for middle school children and articles on ecology, historic houses, antiques, and collectibles. In addition to her traveling and writing, she enjoys teaching other people how to write travel articles, and she frequently conducts seminars and classes.

THE ROLE OF THE TRAVEL WRITER   There are several kinds of travel articles. A service article might help readers choose the best luggage or give tips on how to travel with pets. A destination piece will take a general look at a city or country, giving information on how to get there and suggesting sights, restaurants, and hotels. A third type of article zooms in on a specific angle, such as the architecture or history of a district, a famous person who might have lived there, or an unusual local event.

A travel writer uses every opportunity to find something of interest to document. Even an event or neighborhood close to home can provide material for an entertaining story.

HOW CAROL PERRY GOT STARTED   "I've always enjoyed traveling, and wherever I went I kept a detailed journal of my impressions and collected all the brochures and pamphlets the different tourist bureaus or chambers of commerce give out. When the idea to write took hold, the first subject to come to mind was travel writing. My first article was on side trips from

London. I still write about side trips and day trips travelers to a major city can take."

SPECIAL QUALITIES A TRAVEL WRITER SHOULD HAVE   "In addition to a love of travel, travel writers must also love the written word. They have to be skilled writers and must understand what elements make a story special or interesting. Although attending college is not necessary, it's a good place to learn the basics of writing. Writers also improve their craft by attending seminars, lectures, and workshops and by reading what other writers write. Sometimes a travel writer must also know how to take his or her own photographs."

THE UPSIDES   "I love to travel! I've seen the Parthenon in Greece lit up in a spectacular display at night, I've been on whale-watching assignments—you hear this *whoosh* and all of a sudden forty tons of whale comes roaring out of the water next to you and slams back down. It's very exciting seeing those mammoth whales up close in their own environment. Travel writing has allowed me to see and do things I never would have been able to do otherwise. And I've met wonderful people. When you say the magic words, 'I'm a writer,' it's amazing how lovely and helpful people are."

SOME TIPS FOR NEW WRITERS   "Spend a lot of time composing your query letter. That's what grabs an editor's attention. Make your article proposal sound intriguing, interesting. Find your information from your own first-hand experiences or from the information the chamber of commerce or the library can provide. Take your own photographs or ask the tourist bureau to lend you some.

"And if someone has been helpful to you, giving you information for your story, make sure you send a thank-you note."

Writing Nonfiction Books

Writers of nonfiction have a distinct advantage over fiction writers. Each year, more than two nonfiction titles are published for every fiction book. This means that there are more than twice as many opportunities for the beginning nonfiction book writer to break in and get published. In fact, it's probably safe to say that any competent writer with a little market savvy can find a home for his or her writing.

But you might be thinking that a nonfiction writer needs to be experienced in a specialized field of knowledge before he or she could even think about writing a nonfiction book. After all, a fiction writer can rely on imagination; nonfiction writers have to be experts.

Right?

Wrong.

Nonfiction book writers do not have to start out as experts, though many of them end up that way by the time they've finished. In this chapter you will learn how to go about gathering the information you need to propose, write, and publish your nonfiction book.

Where to Start

As with any book, you must start with an idea, a topic that interests you and that you would like to learn more about. The topics nonfiction writers write about cover everything under the sun. Here is just a small sampling of general categories that publishers are interested in.

Autobiography

Biography

Career/Finding a Job

Child Care

Cooking

Dieting

Health/Fitness

History

Hobbies

How-To

Investing and Making Money

New Age/Spiritual

Parenting

Relationships

Self-Help/Psychology

Textbooks

Travel

At this writing, among the current top fifteen bestselling non-fiction books are: three autobiographies, two biographies, one cookbook, one fitness, one history, two politics, one relationship, and four new age/spiritual.

Most of these books have been written by famous people, but that doesn't mean that an unknown, competent writer can't get a foot in the door.

What to Do with Your Idea

First you have to check what's already been written on the subject. You won't get your book published if it only duplicates the information of a hundred other books. However, if your book idea will provide additional or different information from what is currently available—in other words, if your book will fill a gap in the marketplace—then you have a shot at getting it published.

Go to the library and the bookstore to see what's already out there. Note the publishers of similar titles because they might be the ones who will be interested in your book, too. Once you have examined the competing books, you can decide if your idea is still a good one.

The Next Step

Before you write your proposal, which is your entry into a literary agency or a publishing house, you have to make sure you can collect the information you will need to write your book.

If you already are an expert in a particular area—a hobby or form of cooking, for example—then you have a head start. But you will still need factual information to complete your book. Most nonfiction writers use two sources for information: books, articles, and documents on the subject; and interviews with professionals or experts in the field. If you are writing a biography of a famous person, for example, you can study other books written about that person's life, and you can track down and interview people who know that person. If you want to write about gardening, you interview gardeners. If you want to write about money matters, you interview investment counselors, and so on.

Query Letters and Book Proposals

After you've done your initial research—you have your idea, you know what the competition is, and you know how to gather the information you'll need to write the book—you are ready to compose a query letter. This is basically a miniproposal, telling an editor or agent about your book idea, why you think it should be published, who the readers will be, and why you should be the person to write this book. You end your letter by offering to send a full proposal and sample chapters.

The proposal is a longer version of your query letter. it should include a table of contents that shows you know how to organize and present the material for your book, and one or two sample chapters. If the editor or agent likes your proposal, you'll probably be asked to send the completed manuscript. Few first-time writers can land a book contract without a finished book, but it does happen that a good proposal can get you a sale.

Your proposal could also save you the time of writing a book that will never get published. You might learn from the editors or agents that there is no interest in your idea for a number of reasons. Here are some possibilities:

1. There are too many similar books on the same subject.

2. There aren't any current books on the subject, but that's because earlier ones did not sell well.

3. The audience for your book is too narrow—not enough people would be interested in it to make publishing it financially worthwhile.

4. Your book doesn't cover enough ground.

5. Your book covers too much ground.

If your book idea should be turned down, don't get discouraged. The feedback you get from agents and editors can give you an idea how to revise your book, or it might even lead you to a new topic altogether.

The Rewards for the Nonfiction Book Writer

If you do receive that exciting phone call or letter in the mail informing you your book has been accepted, you can expect to receive a book contract that will spell out all the terms. Usually an advance for a nonfiction book could be from $1,000 up—to even a million dollars or more, depending on how big the publishing house is, how timely and important your book topic is, and how many books the publishers believe they'll be able to sell. First-time writers should expect to fall somewhere at the bottom of the scale.

You will also be paid royalties, a percentage of the price of each book that sells, once the royalties accumulated exceed the amount of your advance. But while you're waiting for your advance or first royalty check, it would be a good idea to get started on that next book. Few people can retire after one book; most writers have to write many in order to support themselves. But writing a complete book, then getting it published, no matter the amount you're paid, is an accomplishment to be proud of, a reward unto itself.

What It's Really Like

Jan Goldberg, Author and Freelance Writer

Jan Goldberg has a B.A. in education from Roosevelt University in Chicago. Her articles have seen print in more than two hundred publications, including *Complete Woman*, *Opportunity Magazine*, *Chicago Parent*, and the Pioneer Press group. She is the author of several books published by VGM Career Horizons, including: *Careers in Journalism*, *Opportunities in Horticulture Careers*, *Opportunities in Research and Development*, *Opportunities in Entertainment*, *Careers for Adventurous Types and Other Go-Getters*, and *On the Job: Real People Working in Communications*. She is also codeveloper of the On the Job series.

HOW JAN GOLDBERG GOT STARTED   "Writing was always my first love. My grandfather was a bookbinder, so as a little girl my sister and brother and I would make trips to his workplace on weekends, which was a special treat. I was so enthralled by the excitement of it—with colored pages and scraps of paper and books that seemed to be piled up to the sky—and the smell of it. I can still remember it and I know that I made up my mind then I would do something with books and writing.

"I'm certified to teach K–12, and I taught for several years, but still it was always the writing that interested me. I started with poetry, then did book reviews for a while.

"I thought about doing some educational writing and made contacts at Scott Foresman and Addison Wesley and then started doing projects for them. I was doing textbook projects and activity workbooks, and more and more I decided I preferred the writing to the teaching.

"Then I contacted an educational publisher that did magazines, and I began to write for *Modern Health* and particularly *Career World*. From there I went in two different directions. I started writing books for VGM Career Horizons and branched out to other publications as well.

"I really enjoyed teaching, and it was a tough call for me, but I've established myself now and I'll stay with the writing. It's a good combination, though: writing and teaching."

THE WRITING LIFE   "I consider my job to be among the most interesting jobs you could find, especially since I write both articles and books in a variety of subject areas. I'm constantly researching new subjects and learning something new. I feel as if I'm an explorer venturing into new territory every time I approach a new topic.

"I certainly never get bored. Right now, for instance, I'm completing a VGM career book and rewriting and revising a Camp Fire activity book, and I have three career articles I've already been assigned.

"This week I also attended a writers' conference, so that means my next project will be to follow up on the contacts I made with several magazine editors there. I'll be putting together my resume and published clips of my articles as samples of my writing.

"A typical days consists of doing many things: the actual writing; keeping in touch with editors; doing research, which might mean going out to the library or some other particular place; or phoning in inquiries about various things.

"Everything I do, I do with an eye to the future. What projects will I be working on in three months from now, in six months from now, even a year from now? So I'm always planning and always at different stages with different projects.

"The good part of all of this is that I can call my own shots and make my own schedule. The bad part is the same, because in order to meet my obligations and do a good job, I really do have to put in a lot of time. Some days could be twelve-hour days, and others, depending on deadlines and how many projects I have going on, I might be able to take some time off. Because I work in a home office, I can work whenever I want—but of course, because the work is always there, I never quite get away from it.

"Also, as a freelancer, you're self-employed, basically running your own business. You have to send out bills, keep good records, have several filing systems, and of course you have to know how to market and sell yourself well. You're doing everything any small business person would do.

"What I like the most is the anticipation of new projects, new ideas, being allowed to be creative and doing new things. But writing is hard work—which a lot of people don't realize—and sometimes it isn't always a lot of fun.

"For me, though, the most difficult part is negotiating contracts and trying to collect money that's owed to me."

SOME TIPS FROM JAN GOLDBERG "You need to have a lot of projects going on at one time if you're going to make a living being a book author or freelance writer. As a novice, you have to be patient or you'll never make it. It's a slow process getting established. You have to pay your dues as in any other profession. You have to be persistent, and it requires a lot of discipline. And you can't really expect too much too soon.

"I've never really figured out an hourly wage for myself, but writing in general is not a high-paying profession. If you want to really make tons of money, you'd probably want to choose another career. Before you think about quitting your day job, you need to be sure how much money you'll be able to make to support yourself."

Jim Haskins, Biographer

Jim Haskins is in the middle of a very distinguished career, with 101 published books to his credit, one of which is *The Cotton Club*, the book that inspired the movie. His interests range from biography and music to history and language. He is also a full professor in the English department of the University of Florida in Gainesville.

HOW JIM HASKINS GOT STARTED   "In a way, I just fell into it. I didn't grow up thinking I wanted to be a writer—it's something I just did. I found I have a knack for it. Nothing drew me to writing; there were no influences, no Fitzgeralds or Hemingways.

"My first book wasn't really a book, it was a diary—*Diary of a Harlem Schoolteacher*. I wasn't planning to teach elementary school for more than one year, and I wanted to keep a diary for my own sake. It ended up being a book because I knew someone who worked in publishing. She had a look and saw its potential."

DOING THE RESEARCH   "If the subjects are agreeable, I'll interview them, and in some cases when they won't do it, other people—family and friends who know them—talk to me. The great mistake people make is thinking that if a person is a 'name' you're going to get the story of his life directly from him. But it doesn't always happen that way. For example, with Michael Jackson, I talked to his brothers. I don't think even Barbara Walters could talk to Michael Jackson.

"For the book I wrote on Richard Pryor, I talked to his lawyer, who happens to be my lawyer as well. With Magic Johnson I talked to his mother and his daddy and people who knew him and went to college with him. Stevie Wonder was one of the agreeable ones—I got to talk to him.

"I never tried to write a definitive book about anybody's life. If I finish it in 1993, by 1995 there's a lot more I could add. Books are not newspapers or current affairs; they're out of date as soon as they come out."

SCHEDULING YOUR TIME   "I write in hotels and on airplanes and everywhere else. I don't use computers; I can't think on them. I write in longhand on yellow legal pads, then I type up the manuscript on an old Royal manual. Then someone enters it into the computer for me.

"I have friends all over the country who send me newspaper clippings I might be interested in. I'm not just beginning the process; writing books is an ongoing process. I'm always working on something.

"For me writing is a job and a craft. There's nothing particularly romantic about it. Some days I don't write at all. I have to do a lot of reading and research and absorb it all before I sit down and write. Some days I read, and some days I think about what I want to write, and then when it comes, it comes. I'll sit and do it. That could be two or three o'clock in the morning.

"I only write about people I'm interested in or subjects I want to learn more about, and when I'm researching one subject I'll come across some interesting information that will lead me to the next project. *Scott Joplin* led into *The Cotton Club*, *The Cotton Club* led into the next one, and so on."

THE UPSIDES   "I like that I have the freedom to do it, the leisure. Reading and writing are luxuries of the leisure class. You can't be a writer unless you're a reader. And you can't be a reader unless you have the time. One hopes that eventually you'll earn enough money to support yourself, but starting out you have to have money. If not, the wolf is always at the door, but you're willing to risk its being there. It's always hand-to-mouth. That's why a lot of writers do a lot of other things besides write."

Further Reading

The following publications provide a wealth of advice on where and how to submit your work and how to survive as a freelance writer.

Children's Writer's and Illustrator's Market, Writer's Digest Books. This annual guide can help aspiring writers and artists to make sure their submissions end up on the right desk. It contains nearly seven hundred markets, including children's book publishers, magazines, scriptwriting markets, greeting card companies, and markets for writing and artwork by children.

Guide to Literary Agents & Art/Photo Reps, Writer's Digest Books. In addition to its more than five hundred listings of fee-charging and nonfee-charging agents and what they handle, this annual guide also showcases several articles of interest to writers.

How to Write a Book Proposal, by Michael Larsen, Writer's Digest Books.

How to Write and Sell Your First Nonfiction Book, by Oscar Collier with Frances Spatz Leighton, St. Martin's Press.

How to Write Irresistible Query Letters, by Lisa Collier Cool, Writer's Digest Books.

Novel & Short Story Writer's Market, Writer's Digest Books. This annual guide provides more than nineteen hundred entries of fiction publishing opportunities, including big publishing houses, small presses, consumer magazines, and literary and

small-circulation magazines. The guide also offers advice and
inspiration from top editors and authors.

Writer's Digest Magazine, P.O. Box 2124, Harlan, IA 51593-
2313. This monthly publication covers every aspect of the
writing life, from magazine queries and articles to poetry,
fiction, and nonfiction. It's an excellent way to learn about all
the different writing options.

Writer's Market, Writer's Digest Books. This annual guide lists
book publishers, magazines, and other publications to which
writers can sell their work. It also includes several articles
offering advice about various aspects of freelance writing.

CHAPTER THREE

Artists

As an artist, you probably hope to carve a niche for yourself in a job that allows you to use your talents. There are a lot of choices, however, and the aim of this chapter is to help you narrow them down and find the career path that best suits your education, interests, and skills.

Within the many job titles open to artists, the following two allow you the most independence: studio artist and freelance commercial artist. Although artists also work in art education, galleries, or museums, those settings, by their very nature, preclude the opportunity of working alone. More information about careers in those settings can be found in the books named at the end of the chapter and from the professional associations listed in the Appendix.

Studio Artists

Your artistic talent has been practiced and honed through your art degree program and through your own hard work. Your goal has always been to support yourself as an artist or craftsperson, perhaps even to open your own studio, a place in which to create and sell your work. Whether it's pottery or painting, sewing or stained glass, you can make a name for yourself and work full-time in your chosen area—without necessarily starving in an artist's garret.

Having said that, few studio artists can move immediately into a career that provides adequate financial support. It takes time to build a reputation or a clientele, and during those "lean years," many artists seek out additional avenues that can assure a regular paycheck.

Although some artists might fall into a variety of moonlighting occupations—anything from food service to secretarial work—the vast majority choose to stay in related fields. Those with a teaching certification may teach art in elementary or secondary schools, while those with master's or doctoral degrees may teach in colleges or universities.

Some fine artists work in arts administration in city, state, or federal arts programs. Others may work as art critics, art consultants, or as directors or representatives in fine art galleries; give private art lessons; or serve as curators setting up art exhibits in museums. You will find talented artists working in a variety of settings, many of which are covered in this chapter.

For the serious studio artist, the main goal is to create a work of art that combines and allows for the need for self-expression and the need to make a living. It can be done.

Fine artists advance as their work circulates and as they establish a reputation for a particular style. The best artists continue to grow in ideas, and their work constantly evolves over time.

Visual Artists

Visual artists, which includes studio (or fine) artists and illustrators, use an almost limitless variety of methods and materials to communicate ideas, thoughts, and feelings. They use oils, watercolors, acrylics, pastels, magic markers, pencils, pen and ink, silk screen, plaster, clay, or any of a number of other media, including computers, to create abstract and realistic works, or images of objects, people, nature, topography, or events.

Whether an artist creates abstract or realistic works depends not so much on the medium, but on the artist's purpose in creating a work of art. Fine artists often create art to satisfy their own need for self-expression, and they may display their work in museums, corporate collections, art galleries, and private homes. Some of their work may be done on request from clients, but not as exclusively as that of graphic artists. (See the section on graphic artists later in this chapter.)

Studio artists usually work independently, choosing whatever subject matter and medium suits them. Usually, they specialize in one or two forms of art.

- *Painters* generally work with two-dimensional art forms. Using techniques of shading, perspective, and color mixing, painters produce works that depict realistic scenes or abstractions that may evoke different moods and emotions, depending on the artists' goals.

- *Sculptors* design three-dimensional art works either by molding and joining materials such as clay, glass, wire, plastic, or metal, or by cutting and carving forms from plaster, wood, or stone. Some sculptors work with mixed media, combining materials such as concrete, metal, wood, plastic, or paper.

- *Potters* work with a variety of clay materials—from low-fire clays to high-fire stoneware or porcelain—and either hand build their artwork or create different forms using a potter's wheel. They follow existing glaze recipes or experiment with different chemicals to formulate their own.

- *Printmakers* create printed images from designs cut into wood, stone, or metal, or from computer-driven data. The designs may be engraved, as in the case of woodblocking, etched, as in the production of etchings, or derived from computers in the form of ink-jet or laser prints, among other techniques.

- *Stained glass artists* work with glass, paints, leading, wood, and other materials to create functional as well as decorative artwork such as windows, skylights, or doors.

- *Photographers* use their cameras, lenses, film, and darkroom chemicals the way a painter uses paint and canvas. They capture realistic scenes of people, places, and events, or through the use of various techniques, both natural and contrived, they create photographs that elicit a variety of moods and emotions.

Training for Studio Artists

In the fine arts field, formal training requirements do not exist, but it is very difficult to become skilled enough to make a living without some basic training. Bachelor's and graduate degree programs in fine arts are offered in many colleges and universities.

In addition to the skills learned or honed, art majors make important contacts during their formal training years. Instructors are often working artists with hands-on experience and advice to offer.

Career Outlook for Studio Artists

The fine arts field has a glamorous and exciting image. Many people with creative ability and a love for drawing qualify for entry to this field. As a result, keen competition can be expected for both salaried jobs and freelance work, especially in fine arts. However, employment of fine artists is expected to grow because of population growth, rising incomes, and growth in the number of people who appreciate fine arts.

Despite the expected employment growth, the supply of those seeking entry to this field will continue to exceed requirements. Fine artists, in particular, may find it difficult to earn a living solely by selling their artwork. Nonetheless, graphic arts studios, clients, and galleries alike are always on the lookout for artists who display outstanding talent, creativity, and style. Talented artists who have developed a mastery of artistic techniques and skills should continue to be in great demand.

What It's Really Like

What better way to learn how to go about starting your career as a professional artist than to hear it from someone who found a way to make a success of it?

Jim Anderson, Stained Glass Artist

Over the past twenty years, Jim Anderson has established himself as a successful stained glass artist in Boston. His studio on Tremont Street in the revitalized South End neighborhood is called Anderson Glass Arts. He attended Boston Museum School of Fine Arts and Massachusetts College of Art and graduated with a B.F.A. and a teaching certificate.

"I started drawing and painting when I was young; even in my baby book it says stuff like 'Jimmy is creative,' 'Jimmy is artistic,' 'Jimmy can draw.' It's one of the areas where I got affirmation as a child.

"I found that I really loved the combination of art and architecture, as opposed to paintings that just hang on walls. I liked the fact that stained glass becomes a permanent part of a building—it becomes architectural art.

"My designs range to all kinds of styles—traditional as well as contemporary. I do hand-painted glass like what you see in churches, and I do styles from different periods—Victorian, Federal, Edwardian, all periods.

"Even as a kid I remember looking at church windows—just staring at them when I was in church. Little did I know that I'd be making them when I got older. I did my first church when I was twenty-six, St. George's Greek Orthodox Church in Hyannis. Now I'm amazed at that kind of undertaking for such a young man. I remember that my colleagues in New York and other places were astounded that the commission for a church was given to such a young artist."

HOW JIM ANDERSON GOT STARTED   "After the Boston Museum School, I went to Massachusetts College of Art to pursue a teaching certificate because I was afraid I wouldn't be able to support myself as an artist and I wanted something to fall back on. But during that time, I realized that I was already actually supporting myself. I started making windows for people, and it paid my way through school.

"Commissions started coming because people saw the work I did on my own house. I own a brownstone in the South End, which is the largest Victorian neighborhood in America with over two thousand structures intact, bowfronts and brownstones.

"I set up a workshop on the ground level of the townhouse so I'd have a place to work, then I did my doorways first. Other neighbors saw them and really loved them. Some of my neighbors were professional architects, and they asked if I'd do their doors. Then other people saw the work and it mushroomed. Over the years I've done ten or fifteen doors on my street alone, and then other people on different streets started seeing them and hiring me.

"Then, before I knew it, someone wrote an article about me in the *Boston Globe,* then in other papers, then Channel Two did a documentary on revitalizing an old art form that included my work. At that point I started getting more and more work. I moved my studio out of my house to a more visible commercial area. I wanted to be able to keep my work on display in the windows.

"Now I have a couple of assistants, one to help me, one to do repair and restoration work. How many assistants I have depends on the economy and how much work I have. As things improve I take on assistants, but if things drop off, I have to let them go. I always make sure there's enough work for at least myself, but now it's doing well, so I can afford to hire help.

"I like going to people's houses and making beautiful windows they really love and that I feel are appropriate for their homes. I wouldn't put a modern window in a Victorian, for example; it wouldn't be suitable.

"I meet a lot of interesting people in my work. Maybe it's because it's an unusual art form and it's usually interesting people who want it.

"The work is fun and challenging and I'm always learning something new. The older I get, the more complicated and sophisticated the commissions get."

THE FINANCES INVOLVED "Money doesn't come in regularly, but it always seems to come in—sometimes in big chunks, sometimes in little chunks. I never know when or what, but I haven't starved and I haven't not paid my bills yet."

SOME ADVICE FROM JIM ANDERSON "Follow your dream, listen to your gut on what to do. Visualize what you want for yourself, then slowly go toward it.

"But start slowly. In my first studio, I made worktables out of plywood and other basic, simple things I could find—nothing fancy or expensive—whatever I could scavenge. I've refined the space over time. Don't spend too much as you go along; let your business build up and don't overextend yourself.

"How important the location of your studio is depends on the art form. If you're a painter, your aim would be to be shown in galleries, so it doesn't matter so much where your studio is. But for other art forms, such as stained glass, it would.

"There are cooperative buildings for artists in lots of major cities now. It's nice to work around other artists and share old warehouse space. It gives you a lot of exposure, plus it keeps you in the art community and the rents are usually reasonable.

"Just work hard and keep an eye on every aspect of the business, including the bookkeeping."

Earnings for Visual Artists

The gallery and artist predetermine how much each earns from a sale. Only the most successful fine artists are able to support themselves solely through sale of their works, however. Most fine artists hold other jobs as well.

Earnings for self-employed visual artists vary widely. Those struggling to gain experience and a reputation may be forced to charge what amounts to less than the minimum wage for their work. Well-established fine artists may earn much more from the sale of their work than salaried artists, but self-employed artists do not receive benefits such as paid holidays, sick leave, health insurance, or pensions.

Working Conditions for Studio Artists

Artists generally work in art and design studios located in commercial space or in their own home studios. Some artists prefer to work alone; others prefer the stimulation of other artists nearby. For the latter group, sharing space with other artists is often a viable alternative to the lone studio—both for camaraderie and for economics. The trend in many large cities, and even in more out-of-the-way areas, is toward shared space in cooperatively owned studios or in rented space in converted warehouses or storefronts.

Artists generally require well-lighted and well-ventilated surroundings because some art forms create odors and dust from glues, paint, ink, clay, or other materials.

Although most fine artists are usually self-employed, working in their own studios, they still depend on stores, galleries, museums, and private collectors as outlets for their work. Others have what many consider to be the ideal situation—a working studio and storefront combined. Still others follow the art fair circuit, packing up their work to tour the country on a regular basis, deriving most if not all of their income from this source alone.

However, many artists will tell you that any of the above options can be risky, with no guarantee of sales. The art fair circuit, in particular, can be unreliable, vulnerable to the vagaries of the weather and the whims of impulse buyers or true art lovers and collectors.

Artisans

There are myriad art and craft forms, and a word should be said here about the prudence of combining the two in a chapter dedicated to artists. There are some who would debate whether "crafts" are true art; however, serious quilters, basket weavers, woodworkers, and all the other artisans who work with their hands to create pleasing and commercially accepted works of art face the same challenges in making a living as do fine painters or sculptors. For those who prefer the stability of job security and a dependable income, there is another setting that should be noted where artists and artisans may create their art and be gainfully employed while they do so, either in a full- or part-time capacity.

Living History Museums

A living history museum is a vibrant, active village, town, or city where the day-to-day life of a particular time period has been authentically re-created. Once you step through the gates, you leave the present behind. The houses and public buildings are restored originals or thoroughly researched reproductions. Interiors are outfitted with period furniture, cookware, bed linens, and tablecloths. Peek under a bed and you might even find a two- or three-hundred-year-old mousetrap.

Colonial Williamsburg in Virginia and Plimoth Plantation in Massachusetts are just two examples of living history museums. Addresses of these and others can be found at the end of this chapter.

These large enterprises offer employment for professional and entry-level workers in a wide variety of categories. Those positions that would be of particular interest to art majors are costumers and artisans in the historic trades.

Most living history museums employ skilled artisans to demonstrate early crafts and trades. Some of these artisans perform in the first-person, playing the role of a particular character of the time. Others wear twentieth-century clothing and discuss their craft from a modern perspective.

Residents in living history museums wear the clothing of the day and discuss their dreams and concerns with visitors as they go about their daily tasks. If you were to stop a costumed gentleman passing by and ask where the nearest McDonald's is, he wouldn't have any idea what you were talking about—unless he thought to direct you to a neighbor's farm. He might even do so using the dialect of his home country.

In the stores and workshops lining the Duke of Gloucester and Francis Streets in Colonial Williamsburg, you will find harness makers, milliners, tailors, needleworkers, silversmiths, apothecaries, candle makers, bookbinders, printers, and wig makers. In the Pilgrim Village and Crafts Center at Plimoth Plantation, coopers, blacksmiths, joiners (cabinetmakers), potters, basket makers, and weavers are re-creating items from the year 1627, seven years after the *Mayflower* landed at Plymouth Rock. Most of the items the pilgrims used in 1627 were brought with them on the *Mayflower* or imported later. Because the Pilgrim Village at Plimoth Plantation is time specific to the year 1627, only those crafts that were practiced then are demonstrated. In addition to their principal occupation as farmers, 1627 pilgrims were coopers, blacksmiths, thatchers, and house builders. The interpretive artisans perform in costume and play the role of a designated pilgrim documented to have lived in Plymouth during that year.

In addition to doing demonstrations, artisans often produce many of the items used on display in the various exhibits. These items include the furniture, cookware, and sometimes even the actual buildings.

What It's Really Like

Tom Gerhardt, a Cooper at Plimoth Plantation

Tom Gerhardt interprets the character of one of the most famous pilgrims, John Alden. Alden was a cooper who worked both inside a one-room cottage he shared with his wife and two children and in the adjoining yard.

Tom talks about his job: "I make barrels and other different-sized wooden containers, such as buckets and churns, while answering visitors' questions about life in seventeenth-century Plymouth.

"Although in Europe you could still find people practicing the craft as it once was done, there are only a few barrel makers in this country. Wooden barrels are made mostly for the wine and spirits industry, but now it's a mechanized craft using power tools and machinery. The finished product is the same as the old craft, but the method is different. We practice the craft as it was done in the 1600s, using only hand tools.

"In addition to my duties as an interpretive cooper, I am also responsible for general woodworking. I am one of several pilgrims building a new house on the grounds.

"What I enjoy most about Plimoth Plantation is that there are a number of very creative and talented people here. If you're willing to do the work, you can learn a good deal for yourself, while at the same time you're educating the visitors.

"There are so many people who will help you—you can be inspired by what they're doing; and you have the time to explore and develop your skills."

TOM GERHARDT'S BACKGROUND   Tom Gerhardt's interest in history began as a small child. His father was a volunteer in charge of a small museum in Virginia, and on vacations he took the family all over the country visiting other museums. It was on one of these trips Tom first discovered Plimoth Plantation.

Later, Tom took a few courses under a master cooper in Portsmouth, New Hampshire, and went to college for a couple of years, studying general liberal arts and theater. He worked in the technical end of theater for a while but decided he wanted a change. Since he'd always been interested in the re-creation of history, in 1985 he returned to Plimoth Plantation and applied for a job as an interpreter.

Deb Mason, a Potter in the Crafts Center

Plimoth Plantation also operates the Crafts Center, where other seventeenth-century crafts are demonstrated. Potters, joiners, basket makers, weavers, and a gift shop share space in a converted carriage house. Artisans in the Crafts Center wear twentieth-century clothing and discuss their work from a modern viewpoint.

In the Crafts Center at Plimoth Plantation, four different potters demonstrate the art of seventeenth-century throwing techniques, though only one potter is on duty at a time. They also make all the pieces that are used in Pilgrim Village by the interpreters. During the winter months when the museum is closed to visitors, the potters make enough items to replenish their stock.

In addition to her own home studio, where she teaches pottery classes, does commission work, and makes pieces for display at various galleries, Deb Mason spends two eight-hour days a week in the Crafts Center and is the supervisor of the other potters.

"In the Crafts Center we don't claim to be seventeenth-century people because pottery wasn't done in the village in 1627," Deb explains. "But because of this, we have an advantage. We can talk to visitors in a way that's totally different from the interpreters. A visitor might go to the village, then come back to the Crafts Center to ask a question that the seventeenth-century interpreters couldn't answer. The interpreters have to speak as though they are pilgrims. They wouldn't have any knowledge beyond 1627.

"For now we are working with twentieth-century equipment, though we are discussing the possibility of going back in time, using a kick wheel and a wood-burning stove. The electric wheels we use now might make throwing look faster and easier than it was in the seventeenth-century, but the techniques are still very much the same.

"The difference is we have to make only period pieces, and that's where some of the difficulties come in. For example, we're trying to find the right clay bodies to work with. We have a few original pieces on display to study, and you can see the clay color and texture. We've been experimenting, trying to develop clay bodies that are close to the original.

"That's been fairly successful, but we're having a tough time with glazes. They used a lot of lead back then. In fact, most every glaze was lead based. Because we sell the pieces we make in the gift shop and they're also used in the village every day, we've been trying to get away from lead. It's hard to come up with glazes that have the same shine and the same colors; lead has a very typical look. We're using a ground glass that melts at a low temperature, which is a characteristic of lead and produces similar results.

"We make ointment pots that held salves and other healing lotions, apothecary jars, bowls, porringers for porridge, oil lamps, candlesticks, and pipkins—little cooking pots with a side handle and three little legs on the bottom. We also make a lot of three-handled cups. Pilgrims usually shared their eating implements. The cups are funny-looking things—a popular item in the craft shop.

"Back then the pottery was hastily thrown. There's a real earthy quality to the pieces. Their perception of what was beautiful and what was utilitarian was different. What they strove for was extremely rough by today's standards.

"My biggest problem is remembering not to throw too well. The advantage to that, though, for potters wanting to work here, is that a high degree of skill is not necessary."

DEB MASON'S BACKGROUND   Deb Mason earned her B.A. in art with a major in ceramics in 1973 from Bennington College in Vermont. She taught ceramics full-time for thirteen years at a private school and was the head of the art department her last few years there. She joined the staff at Plimoth Plantation in 1992.

Patricia Baker, a Costumer at Plimoth Plantation

Most living history museums employ professional costumers to keep their character interpreters and presenters outfitted in authentic period clothing. Costumers generally work behind the scenes reproducing the apparel the average inhabitant would have worn.

Patricia Baker is Wardrobe and Textiles Manager at Plimoth Plantation. Her office and work space occupy a section of a converted dairy barn on the grounds of the museum. The atmosphere is that of a cozy living room with a lot of shelves and fabrics draped here and there, sewing machines and rocking chairs, a large cutting table, garment racks, and a radio.

"The clothes my department makes are common to what the middle class would have worn," she explains. "We provide our interpreters with enough clothing so they can dress authentically from the skin out. They don't even have to wear modern underwear if they don't want to.

"The basic undergarment for both men and women is a shift. It's a long, linen, T-shaped garment that reaches to the knees. Over that the men wear breeches and a doublet, a close-fitting jacket that comes to just above the waist. The breeches are tied into the jacket by laces.

"Women wear a plain corset over their shifts. It gives them a smooth, cone-shaped look. Next comes a number of petticoats and skirts and a padded roll to enhance the hips. Waistlines are raised and meet in a point.

"We use wool and linen and a little cotton, all naturally dyed. We try to duplicate the same materials used in the seventeenth-century, as well as the same construction techniques. Much of the sewing is done by hand.

"We also make all the household furnishings that are used for display in the various exhibits. These are the seventeenth-century equivalents to what we have in the twentieth-century: sheets, pillow cases (called *pillow beres*), feather and straw beds, paneled bed curtains, tablecloths, napkins, and cupboard cloths.

"Maintaining and repairing existing costumes and furnishings are also part of our duties, as well as conducting as much research as possible to keep our creations accurate for the particular time period.

"Because there are so few surviving garments—conditions were very harsh in those early years—we look to different sources— paintings, engravings, woodcuts, written descriptions, wills, inventories, diaries, and plays.

"We also study the few remaining garments on display in different museums through our extensive slide collection of styles and techniques. Most of those museums are in England, the Victoria and Albert, or the Museum of Costumes in Bath, for example. The clothing seems to have had a better survival rate over there."

PATRICIA BAKER'S BACKGROUND   Patricia graduated from the Massachusetts College of Art in 1976 with a bachelor of fine arts degree in crafts. Her concentration was in fabrics and fibers. She immediately began work at Plimoth Plantation as a character interpreter. In 1985 she joined the wardrobe department and became its head the following year.

Joel Pontz, a Joiner in the Crafts Center

Joel Pontz supervises all interpretive artisans at Plimoth Plantation as well as a character interpreter for the farmer John Adams. He also demonstrates his joinery skills in the Crafts Center.

Joel describes his job: "I step back and forth between the seventeenth and the twentieth centuries. Several days a week I'm in costume in the village as John Adams, picking my share of rutabagas or building small animal shelters or fences. On the other days I'm in modern clothing in the Crafts Center, demonstrating joinery.

"Joiners were the principle furniture makers of the period, in the age before cabinetry. We use different kinds of saws and edged hand tools, such as axes, planes, gimlets, and augers, rather than power tools. If we want to reproduce the right texture or style, we have to be purists about it.

"In the Craft Center, in front of the public or behind the scenes, we make furniture for the village—large cupboards, bedsteads, chairs, mousetraps, and children's toys. We don't want to demonstrate any crafts in the village section of the museum that weren't practiced at the time. It would be anachronistic."

JOEL PONTZ'S BACKGROUND   Joel Pontz grew up nearby and started at Plimoth Plantation as a volunteer pilgrim after school and on weekends. In 1973 he became a full-time interpreter. He learned his joinery skill on site from the other staff members and the research department.

"I hated woodworking in school," Joel admits. "It wasn't until I started working at the plantation using hand tools and trying to decipher how things were made that it became actually interesting for me. The historical aspect of it was what fascinated me. If it were just doing straight carpentry, I probably wouldn't have stayed with it."

Joel advises taking a few courses in historic trades or historic preservation. "But," he cautions, "the skills we need are particular to Plimoth Plantation. Outside courses would be painted with such a broad brush, but what's done at Plimoth Plantation is very focused on a particular group of people in a very short time span.

"The best qualification would be a lot of hand-tool work. The tools haven't changed that much over the centuries. Try taking a tree and make a table or a chair from it. That's the best way to learn the art."

Job Strategies for Working in Living History Museums

The competition is fairly high for artisan or costumer positions at living history museums. For example, the wardrobe department at Plimoth Plantation is a small one, currently employing only four workers. Other larger living history museums, such as Colonial Williamsburg, need more people. A good way to get a foot in the door is to work as a volunteer or apply for an apprenticeship, internship, or work-study position. Many start out as character interpreters or presenters then move into their chosen position when openings occur. Because of limited budgets and a low turnover, openings are rare.

Salaries for artisans within living history museums differ depending on whether they are full-time or part-time. The latter group earns an hourly wage ranging between $7.50 and $10. A new graduate just starting out full-time could expect to earn in the high-teens to mid-twenties, depending on the location and available funding.

Commercial Artists

Commercial artists, also known as graphic artists, and illustrators put their artistic skills and vision at the service of commercial clients, such as major corporations, retail stores, and advertising, design, or publishing firms. Their lot in life is much more secure than that of the studio artist, although a regular paycheck doesn't always guarantee the artistic freedom the former group enjoys.

Graphic artists, whether freelancers or employed by a firm, use a variety of print, electronic, and film media to create art that meets a client's needs. Graphic artists are increasingly using computers instead of the traditional tools such as pens, pencils, scissors, and color strips to produce their work. Computers enable them to lay out and test various designs, formats, and colors before printing a final design.

The Role of the Graphic Artist

Graphic artists perform different jobs depending on their area of expertise and the needs of their employers. Some work for only one employer; other graphic artists freelance and work for a variety of clients.

- *Graphic designers* may create packaging and promotional displays for a new product, the visual design of an annual report and other corporate literature, or a distinctive logo for a product or business. They also help with the layout and design of magazines, newspapers, journals, and other publications, and create graphic images for television.

- *Illustrators* paint or draw pictures for books, magazines, and other publications, films, and paper products, including greeting cards, calendars, wrapping paper, and stationery. Many do a variety of illustration formats, while others specialize in a particular style.

- *Medical and scientific illustrators* combine artistic skills with knowledge of the biological sciences. Medical illustrators make detailed renderings of human anatomy and surgical procedures. Scientific illustrators draw illustrations of animals and plants. These illustrations are used in medical and scientific publications and in audiovisual presentations for teaching purposes. Medical illustrators also work for lawyers, producing exhibits for court cases, and for doctors.

- *Fashion artists* draw illustrations of women's, men's, and children's clothing and accessories for magazines, newspapers, and other media.

- *Story board artists* draw the plans for TV commercials. Story boards present TV commercials in a series of scenes similar to a comic strip so an advertising client (the company doing the advertising) can evaluate proposed commercials. Story boards may also serve as guides to placement of actors and cameras and to other details during the production of commercials.

- *Cartoonists* draw political, advertising, social, and sports cartoons. Some cartoonists work with others who create the idea or story and write the captions. Most cartoonists, however, have humorous, critical, or dramatic talents in addition to drawing skills.

- *Animators* work in the motion picture and television industries. They draw by hand and use computers to create the large series of pictures that, when transferred to film or tape, form the animated cartoons seen in movies and on TV.

- *Art directors*, also called *visual journalists*, read the material to be printed in periodicals, newspapers, and other printed media and decide how to visually present the information in an eye-catching yet organized manner. They make decisions about which photographs or artwork to use and in general oversee production of the printed material.

Working Conditions for Graphic Artists

Graphic artists work in art and design studios located in office buildings or their own homes. Graphic artists employed by publishing companies and art and design studios generally work a standard forty-hour week. During busy periods, they may work overtime to meet deadlines.

Self-employed graphic artists can set their own hours, but they may spend much time and effort selling their services to potential customers or clients and establishing a reputation.

What It's Really Like

Peggy Peters, Freelance Illustrator

Peggy Peters teaches art at an alternative school in Texas. She also works as a freelance illustrator. "As my undergraduate degree was in fine arts, not graphic arts, it was difficult to make the transition to commercial art," she says. "Where I lived there were no schools with graphic arts majors, and I didn't really know the field.

"I felt considerably handicapped trying to succeed in this profession. Fortunately, I went for my master's at Syracuse University and earned my degree in illustration. The degree program was unique. It was through the independent studies department and only working illustrators were accepted into the program. My group consisted of about sixteen people—illustrators from Alaska, Canada, California, England, Arizona, New York, Virginia, all over. I gained a broad overview of the profession, and the program was specifically geared to career development. I feel much more prepared now.

"My commercial art experience began in junior high when I sold Beatles portraits. I was a set designer for public television, and I had my own studio for executing portraits and various commissioned works.

"Now I am beginning to sell illustrations locally, working specifically with fine arts organizations, theaters, the opera, etc. I am also doing all the art work for the World Flight project in which a local pilot, Linda Finch, plans to duplicate exactly the flight of Amelia Earhart.

"Currently I am also seeking a limited number of illustration jobs to build a portfolio. Because I am teaching full-time, both to keep health insurance and to pay off my student loan for my master's program, I cannot seek lots of jobs. I go to local theater and fine arts organizations to see if they would like to develop graphics for advertising—posters, illustrations for products to raise funds, cups, T-shirts, that sort of thing. In a year I plan to show my work to someone who does many of the Broadway show posters.

"And I'm learning computer graphics. In the last ten years or so, three-fourths of all illustration and design jobs are done on computer, according to various trade magazines such as *Step-by-Step Graphics*."

SOME ADVICE FROM PEGGY PETERS   "If I knew starting out what I know now I would have saved myself a lot of grief. For a real jump start in the career, go to the best art school possible— Rhode Island School of Design, Chicago Art Institute, Syracuse University, CalArts, Savannah, etc.

"Also, get computer literate now. Learn PageMaker, Quark Xpress, Illustrator, Freehand, some 3-D programs, and learn as much as you can before college.

"Target the type of design or illustration you want to do and study the careers of artists doing things you want to do. Write to a few artists to learn what they did. The days of big advertising design firms are gone. More and more people are working freelance, and you don't have to be in New York City or Chicago to be successful any more. With today's technology, illustrators are living and working everywhere these days.

"There are many different types of illustration or design careers. The best way to succeed is to find out what you really want to do, then go about finding out how to do it. For example, I love performing arts, so my thesis for my M.A. was on Broadway poster illustrators. I found out how the top people in that field—Jim McMullan, Paul Davis, etc.—structured their careers. This gave me some idea as to how I could do this myself and if my ideas were practical at all.

"The field changes rapidly, so flexibility is another important consideration. For example, multimedia was the hot field a few years ago but it already is reaching a saturation point. Only about 5 percent of any multimedia product proves really successful, and the investment to produce a product is very high.

"Temperament is as important as talent. If you must make art to be happy, then you should pursue an arts career, but only if it is an absolute necessity. Being prolific is a great advantage also."

Possible Employers for Graphic Artists

Many graphic artists work part-time as freelancers while continuing to hold a full-time job until they get established. Others have enough talent, perseverance, and confidence in their ability to start out freelancing full-time immediately after they graduate from art school. Many do freelance work part-time while still in school in order to develop experience and a portfolio of published work.

The freelance artist develops a set of clients who regularly contract for work. Some successful freelancers are widely recognized for their skill in specialties such as children's book illustration, design, or magazine illustration. These artists can earn high incomes and can pick and choose the type of work they do.

But more often than not, freelance careers take time to build. While making contacts and developing skills, many find work in various organizations.

Other commercial artists prefer full-time employment over freelancing. They find work in the following settings: advertising agencies, design firms, publishing companies, department stores, television, motion pictures, manufacturing firms, and the various agencies within the local, state, and federal government.

Training and Qualifications

Graphic Arts

In the graphic arts field, demonstrated ability and appropriate training or other qualifications are needed for success. Evidence of appropriate talent and skill shown in the portfolio is an important factor used by art and design directors and others in deciding whether to hire or contract out work to an artist. The portfolio is a collection of handmade, computer-generated, or printed examples of the artist's best work. In theory, a person with a good portfolio but no training or experience could succeed in graphic arts. In reality, assembling a successful portfolio requires skills generally developed in a postsecondary art or design school program, such as a bachelor's degree program in fine art, graphic design, or visual communications.

Internships also provide excellent opportunities for artists and designers to develop and enhance their portfolios. Most programs in art and design also provide training in computer design techniques. This training is becoming increasingly important as a qualification for many jobs in commercial art.

Medical Illustration

The appropriate training and education for prospective medical illustrators is more specific. Medical illustrators must not only demonstrate artistic ability but also have a detailed knowledge of living organisms, surgical and medical procedures, and human and sometimes animal anatomy. A four-year bachelor's degree combining art and premedical courses is usually required, followed by a master's degree in medical illustration, a degree offered in only a few accredited schools in the United States.

Advancement Opportunities

In general, illustrators and designers advance as their work circulates and as they establish a reputation for a particular style. The best illustrators continue to grow in ideas, and their work constantly evolves over time.

Graphic artists may advance to assistant art director, art director, design director, and in some companies, creative director of an art or design department. Some may gain enough skill to succeed as a freelancer or may prefer to specialize in a particular area. Others decide to open their own businesses.

Strategies for Job Hunting

As in any professional career, developing contacts and having a foot in the door at the type of organization for which you'd like to work are valuable assets. Internships are pathways to both. The best strategy is to plan ahead. During your undergraduate or graduate studies, arrange for as many internships as you can squeeze in—either full-time during the summers or part-time during semesters.

Learning how an advertising agency or a public relations firm or a TV studio functions will give you a broad overview and also help you build a successful portfolio. If an internship gave you a foot in the door, a professional and creative portfolio can open that door all the way. In addition, find yourself a mentor, someone who can critique your portfolio and advise you on how best to proceed.

Earnings for Graphic Artists

The average salary for those working in design and graphic arts runs about $25,000, according to the College Placement Council.

According to the Society of Publication Designers, entry-level graphic designers earned between $21,000 and $24,000 annually.

For More Information

The following books provide information on career paths available to artists who also enjoy working with other people:

Great Jobs for Art Majors, by Blythe Camenson (VGM Career Horizons)
Opportunities in Museums, by Blythe Camenson (VGM Career Horizons)

For information about living history museums, contact the following:

Colonial Williamsburg
Employment Office
P.O. Box 1776
Williamsburg, VA 23187

Plimoth Plantation
P.O. Box 1620
Plymouth, MA 02360

St. Augustine's Spanish Quarter
Historic St. Augustine Preservation Board
P.O. Box 1987
St. Augustine, FL 32085

Director of Personnel
Old Sturbridge Village
One Old Sturbridge Village Road
Sturbridge, MA 01566

CHAPTER FOUR

Freelance Researchers

Research—in a variety of subject areas—is a major area of work that allows the freelancer independence. In this chapter you will learn about genealogy as a career and also be introduced to several researchers whose jobs don't fall into any of the expected categories.

Genealogists

The study of genealogy, tracing family histories, has recently become one of the most popular hobbies in the United States. Many people share a keen interest in their family backgrounds. Many genealogy hobbyists take their interest one step further and become self-employed genealogists, helping others to dig up their family trees. Genealogists also are employed in historical societies and libraries with special genealogy rooms.

The Church of Jesus Christ of Latter Day Saints in Salt Lake City, for example, has a huge repository of family information in a subterranean library. The church employs genealogists all over the world and includes genealogists who have been accredited through its own program on a list of freelance researchers. For more information, write to the address listed in the Appendix.

Other genealogists find work teaching their skills to others in adult education classes or by editing genealogy magazines or writing books or newspaper genealogy columns.

Most genealogists are not formally trained, though specializing in genealogy is possible through some university history and library science programs. In addition, genealogists can become board certified. For information on certification requirements and procedures write to the Board for Certification of Genealogists, listed in the Appendix.

Salaries

Salaries vary depending upon the institution where a genealogist is employed and upon the level of expertise he or she has reached. Self-employed genealogists make anywhere from $15 to $35 an hour.

How to Get Started

The National Genealogy Society makes the following suggestions for beginners:

1. *Question older family members*. Encourage them to talk about their childhoods and relatives and listen carefully for clues they might inadvertently drop. Learn good interviewing techniques so you ask questions that elicit the most productive answers. Use a tape recorder and try to verify each fact through a separate source.

2. *Visit your local library*. Become familiar with historical and genealogical publications (a few sources are provided at the end of this chapter and in the Appendix) and contact local historical societies and the state library and archives in your state capital. Seek out any specialty ethnic or religious libraries.

3. *Visit courthouses*. Cultivate friendships with busy court clerks. Ask to see source records such as wills, deeds, marriage books, birth and death certificates. Visiting cemeteries also provides useful information.

4. *Enter into correspondence.* Write to other individuals or societies involved with the same families or regions. Contact foreign embassies in Washington, D.C. Restrict yourself to asking only one question in each letter you send. Include the information you have already uncovered. Include a self-addressed, stamped envelope to encourage replies.

5. *Become computer literate.* Members of the National Genealogical Society can participate in a special computer-interest section. It encourages the use of computers in research, record management, and data sharing.

6. *Keep painstaking records.* Use printed family group sheets or pedigree charts. Develop a well-organized filing system so you'll be able to easily find your information. Keep separate records for each family you research.

7. *Write the National Genealogical Society.* Take advantage of the society's forty-six-page *Beginners in Genealogy* book, charts, and library loan program. You can also enroll in a home study course called *American Genealogy: A Basic Course.*

What It's Really Like

Valarie Neiman, Academic Researcher

Valarie Neiman formed EVN Flow Services in 1993. Through her home-based business she does academic, business, and creative writing and provides research and editing services. She earned her B.S. in business administration in 1980 from Arizona State University, in Tempe and her M.A. in human resources development in 1993 from Ottawa University in Phoenix.

"Research isn't what I do, it's part of who I am," she recalls. "As one of the original latchkey kids in the 1950s, I spent a lot of time reading when I got home from school. To avoid being bored in class, I'd always read ahead in the textbooks. My first job fresh out of high school in 1966 was typing resumes. It's surprising how little they've changed in thirty years. The woman I worked for at the time began letting me write them, and soon, I did the interviews as well.

"After a variety of clerical and secretarial jobs, I went back to school in my midtwenties and earned a bachelor's degree in business. Eventually, while working for a major defense contractor, I began work on a master's. I was excused from the employer who had been paying my tuition and went on to temporary positions— from management consultant back to typist. Bummer!

"My final temp assignment was researching and writing warehouse procedures. I convinced the manager that it would be cheaper to hire me as an independent contractor rather than pay the temp agency. At the same time, I put up a notice at my alma mater offering to help students with their research projects.

"The rest, as they say, is history. When I began EVN Flow (Ellwood and Valarie Neiman keep work flowing), my current business, I expected to help students format and type their papers. However, adult learners (over twenty-five) often haven't had training or don't remember how to write research papers. My work soon evolved into "filling in the gaps" in their abilities. Part of the job is reassuring them that they aren't stupid, letting them know I've developed a unique (and marketable) talent for pulling their work together into a package that makes them look good.

"The work I do is enjoyable because every day is different and every project takes me on a new path. Had I realized years ago that I am what is gently referred to as an 'individual contributor' I may have found my niche sooner. I prefer to work alone, without supervision. I focus on the task at hand and am goal-oriented enough to get it done so I can move to the next project.

"People may think of researchers as scientists or academics. I believe research is an element in almost every job, whether dealing with things, people, or ideas. Most of the time, though, it isn't thought of as research.

"To me, the distinction of a job as a researcher is that the goal is to present knowledge in a different way, consolidate facts and assemble them to make a point, discover new relationships in existing knowledge, or develop background and authenticity—in creative writing, for example.

"One of the things I like least about my work is that it isn't full-time and can be seasonal. I began writing a novel to fill those dreaded unbillable hours. Of course, the part-time nature of the work is also one of the things I like best! I'm sure that others in various types of research positions make a living. By my own choice, I make enough to pay business expenses and to pay myself a small stipend. Because I am a business, travel, postage, supplies, and capital equipment associated with my writing are all considered expenses.

"My business is home based. I have one employee (my husband), who is financial manager and gofer. We share a large office and one mother-ship computer, and I have an old laptop for plain old writing.

"I tutor adult learners in planning, researching, and writing academic papers. I review and edit master's research and graduation review projects. I am under contract with Ottawa University to read and edit first drafts of master's candidates' theses.

"I also collaborate on research and writing a series of booklets on pricing, niche marketing, networking, outsourcing, tax tips, and how to start a home-based business (published by the Home-Based Business Association of Arizona, HBBA).

"My time is mine to spend as I wish. Since I like variety, and 'big' projects, I find I work for an hour or so on one, then shift to another, and so forth. Some days, I catch up on phone calls or maintenance, but if I have paying clients, I stay focused on them. Some days I work fourteen hours (rare), others only three or four. I have a wonderful, understanding boss."

SOME ADVICE FROM VALARIE NEIMAN "Read, read, read, research, research, research. Go to the library, get on-line, practice finding things. Interview people, create questionnaires, read magazines.

"The key requirement for a life of research is a desire, not to say compulsion, to *know*. In addition, a researcher (whether scientific, academic, or journalistic) needs persistence, judgment, empathy, and intuition. A researcher must establish limits and develop shortcuts or the process goes on forever, each step leading to another source, ad infinitum.

"A researcher with broad experience is more likely to be exposed to a variety of sources—not just the public library. I've worked in government, major corporations, and small businesses. Each job provided a whole new set of resources that I am now able to draw upon.

"How to get a research job? The possibilities are endless, but chances are good there won't be an ad in the newspaper. *Researcher* is more an activity than a job title. It's the same old story. Network, create an excellent resume, and research your prospects.

"A college degree or three is probably a good start (up to and including a Ph.D. or postdoctoral work). The major doesn't matter. A student who thrives in an academic environment will likely have the curiosity and temperament to excel as a researcher.

"With the emphasis on education (to keep youngsters out of the job market as long as possible), even a fact checker at a newspaper or magazine would probably need a degree.

"Hone those writing skills. Research is useless without presenting results. Facts are just data. A researcher worth his or her salt must be able to interpret the facts and consolidate or extrapolate them into usable information.

"And remember, in scientific or social research, especially, the honesty and ethics of a researcher must be unquestioned. A researcher must maintain the confidentiality of people and ideas."

Susan Broadwater-Chen, Information Specialist and Freelance Writer

Susan Broadwater-Chen owns Moonstone Research and Publications, her own home-based business in Charlottesville, Virginia. She has a B.A. in humanities from Asbury College in Wilmore, Kentucky, and an M.A. in theological studies from Emory University in Atlanta, Georgia.

"I have an insatiable curiosity about just about everything, and I love to write," she explains. "I especially like the challenge of having to find something and the excitement that comes when I find it. I love libraries, books, and puzzles, and some of the searches that I do are very much like putting puzzles together.

"I attended Mountain Empire Community college in southwest Virginia in the early 1980s and took as many computer courses, including programming, as were offered. After finishing those courses, I took a job at the University of Virginia as a program support technician, and part of my job was to do a lot of editing and spending a lot of time working with research assistants.

"Eventually I took courses through UVA on how to navigate the Internet and do Web pages. I worked at UVA for ten years and ran a business out of my home, doing everything from research to editing during that time.

"I started in 1986 on a part-time, moonlighting basis. I've been full-time since 1995. I had built up enough contacts and customers that I could become independent. I quit my job at UVA and started publishing a monthly newsletter and running a web page. When I realized that I could support myself by using my skills to expand my client base, I decided to devote myself full-time to this business.

"Currently I publish a monthly newsletter that focuses on Internet materials that writers will find useful. I also take individual research projects from authors who are looking for information that is proving hard for them to find on their own.

"In addition, I work with a couple of on-line author colonies/ work groups in developing content for research libraries. This includes going through antiquarian books, microfilm, and other sources to provide both primary source materials and bibliographical information. My company has a storefront on the Internet where writers or anyone else can download some materials for free and pay for others. I offer a clipping service for subscribers and hold a weekly workshop on-line to help people with any questions they might have about finding what they are looking for.

"The job is very demanding. Most of my customers can't wait a week or two for what they are looking for. In addition, putting out a large newsletter each month and submitting articles to at least one on-line magazine each month is very time consuming. I begin my day at 6:00 A.M. and as my son eats his breakfast I check my E-mail, writing down every request that comes through on a special pad. After that I check the news groups/news services to see if there is anything I need to come back to later and delete what I don't want to look at.

"After I get my son on the bus I come back and print the articles I want to read or save. As soon as that is done I file them in topical folders. You have to be organized in this job or you are doomed to have all kinds of paper and not know how to put your hands on what you really need when you need it. I keep a folder of things I may want to review or talk about in my newsletter and the rest is filed by topic.

"Next I work on the products I intend to sell. This means reading and writing articles or finding out-of-copyright primary source material that can be edited and reprinted for sale. I try to do a minimum number of these products a day.

"After that is finished I turn to the content I am developing for the on-line services. When that is finished it's time to check E-mail again and to start working on the requests I have received overnight. I walk after that because I need time to myself and away from my desk.

"When I come back to work I write at least one review or article for my newsletter and then start exploring potential Internet sources that I may want to review. I take notes and make printouts and put this aside to be written up the next day. Next I Telnet into library card catalogs looking for materials that I may want to request on interlibrary loan from my local library and write down information on those books.

"Because I work at home it's a relaxed atmosphere, but sometimes I feel really pressured because there seems to be so much to do and only a limited number of hours in a day. I usually work about eighty hours a week, which is forty more than when I worked for someone else. I have one morning that I spend in the library every week. The job is not boring, but it's not easy money either.

"I like it when I can help people. It makes me feel good to know that they're happy with what I've found. When I've helped a person who is publishing books and he or she sends me a copy of the book, I get personal satisfaction knowing that I've helped with the research that the book required. I also like the feeling I get when I find some really obscure fact and pull the needle out of the haystack. The downside is that sometimes I can't help people because the facts won't bear out what they want to write about."

SOME ADVICE FROM SUSAN BROADWATER-CHEN   "It's not an easy job. You need to learn all you can about electronic databases and the Internet. In addition, you need to learn all you can about how to find information in your library and from interviewing people.

"You can't have a business based on Internet research alone. You have to cultivate as many skills as possible and know where to look for specific material. It's important to build up a client base and connections before you go full-time. Volunteer for groups that might need your services on the Internet. Submit articles to on-line publications and start networking with people in professions or with interests who might need your services."

CHAPTER FIVE

Computer Professionals

C omputer scientists, systems analysts, and computer programmers all spend at least a major percentage of their
time working alone. Although many projects start off as
a group effort utilizing a team approach, in the end, the actual
work gets done alone.

Computer Scientists and Systems Analysts

The rapid spread of computers and computer-based technologies
over the past two decades has generated a need for skilled, highly
trained workers to design and develop hardware and software systems and to determine how to incorporate these advances into
new or existing systems. Although many narrow specializations
have developed and no uniform job titles exist, these professionals are widely referred to as computer scientists and systems
analysts.

Computer scientists, including computer engineers, conduct
research, design computers, and discover and use principles of
applying computers. Computer scientists and engineers may perform many of the same duties as other computer professionals
throughout a normal workday, but their jobs are distinguished by
the higher level of theoretical expertise they apply to complex
problems and innovative ideas for the creation or application of
new technology.

Computer scientists employed by academic institutions work in areas from theory to hardware to language design, or on multidiscipline projects, such as developing and advancing uses for artificial intelligence (AI). Their counterparts in private industry work in areas such as applying theory, developing specialized languages, or designing programming tools, knowledge-based systems, or computer games. Computer engineers often work as part of a team that designs new computing devices or computer-related equipment.

Far more numerous than scientists and engineers, systems analysts define business, scientific, or engineering problems and design their solutions using computers. This process may include planning and developing new computer systems or devising ways to apply existing systems to operations still completed manually or by some less-efficient method. Systems analysts may design entirely new systems, including hardware and software, or create a single new software application to harness more of the computer's power.

Analysts begin an assignment by discussing the data processing problem with managers and users to determine its exact nature. Much time is devoted to clearly defining the goals of the system so that it can be broken down into separate programmable procedures.

Analysts then use techniques such as structured analysis, data modeling, information engineering, mathematical model building, sampling, and cost accounting to plan the system. Once the design has been developed, systems analysts prepare charts and diagrams that describe it in terms that managers and other users can understand. They may prepare a cost-benefit and return-on-investment analysis to help management decide whether the proposed system will be satisfactory and financially feasible.

Analysts must specify the files and records to be accessed by the system, design the processing steps, and design the format for the output that will meet the users' needs. They must be sure that the system they design is user friendly, so that it can be learned easily by the user and any problems encountered can be overcome quickly. Analysts also ensure security of the data by making it inaccessible to those who are not authorized to use it.

When the system is accepted, systems analysts may determine what computer hardware and software will be needed to set up the system or implement changes to it. They coordinate tests and observe initial use of the system to ensure it performs as planned. They prepare specifications, work diagrams, and structure charts for computer programmers to follow and then work with them to eliminate errors from the system. Some organizations do not employ programmers; instead, a single worker called a programmer-analyst is responsible for both systems analysis and programming. This is becoming more common with the development of Computer Assisted Software Engineering (CASE) tools, which automate much of the coding process, making programming functions easier to learn.

One of the biggest obstacles to wider computer use is the inability of different computers to communicate with each other. Many systems analysts are involved with connecting all the computers in an individual office, department, or establishment. This networking has many variations; it may be called a local area network, a wide area network, or a multiuser system, for example. A primary goal of networking is to allow users of microcomputers (also known as personal computers or PCs) to retrieve data from a mainframe computer and use it on their machines. This connection also allows data to be entered into the mainframe from the PC.

Because up-to-date information, accounting records, sales figures, or budget projections, for example, are so important in modern organizations, systems analysts may be instructed to make the computer systems in each department compatible with each other so facts and figures can be shared. Similarly, electronic mail requires open pathways to send messages, documents, and data from one computer mailbox to another across different equipment and program lines. Analysts must design the gates in the hardware and software to allow free exchange of data, custom applications, and the computer power to process it all. They study the seemingly incompatible pieces and create ways to link them so that users can access information from any part of the system.

Because the possible uses of computers are so varied and complex, analysts usually specialize in either business, scientific, engineering, or microcomputer applications. Previous experience or training in a particular area usually dictates the field in which they are most qualified to develop computer systems.

Computer Programmers

In many large organizations, programmers follow descriptions prepared by systems analysts who have carefully studied the task that the computer system is going to perform. These descriptions list the input required, the steps the computer must follow to process data, and the desired arrangement of the output.

In some organizations, particularly smaller ones, workers called programmer-analysts handle both systems analysis and programming. Programmers in software development companies often work without the contribution of systems analysts. Instead, they may work directly with experts from various fields to create software programs designed either for specific clients or as packaged software for general use, ranging from games and education software to programs for desktop publishing, financial planning, and spreadsheets.

The transition from a mainframe environment to a primarily PC–based environment has brought about a blurring of the once rigid distinction between the programmer and the user. Increasingly adept users are taking over many of the programming tasks previously performed by programmers. For example, the growing use of packaged software, like spreadsheet and database management software packages, allows users to write simple programs to calculate or access data.

Regardless of setting, programmers write specific programs by breaking down each step into a logical series of instructions the computer can follow. They then code these instructions in a conventional programming language, such as C and FORTRAN, or one of the more advanced artificial intelligence or object-oriented languages, such as LISP, Prolog, C++, or Ada.

Much of the programming being done today is for the preparation of packaged software, one of the most rapidly growing segments of the computer industry. Despite the prevalence of packaged software, many programmers are involved in updating, repairing, and modifying code for existing programs. When making changes to a section of code, called a routine, programmers need to make other users aware of the task that the routine is to perform. They do this by inserting comments in the coded instructions so others can understand the program. Programmers using computer-aided software engineering (CASE) can concentrate on writing the unique parts of the program because the computer automates some of the more basic processes. This also yields more reliable and consistent programs and increases programmers' productivity by eliminating some of the routine steps.

When a program is ready to be tested, programmers run the program to ensure that the instructions are correct and will produce the desired information. They prepare sample data that test every part of the program and, after trial runs, review the results to see if any errors were made. If errors do occur, the programmers must change and recheck the program until it produces the correct results. This is called debugging the program.

Finally, programmers working in a mainframe environment prepare instructions for the computer operator who will run the program. They may also contribute to a user's manual for the program.

Programs vary with the type of information to be accessed or generated. For example, the data involved in updating financial records are different from those required to simulate a flight on a pilot trainee's monitor. Although simple programs can be written in a few hours, programs that use complex mathematical formulas or many data files may require more than a year of work. In most cases, several programmers may work together as a team under a senior programmer's supervision.

Programmers often are grouped into two broad types: applications programmers and systems programmers. Applications programmers usually are oriented toward business, engineering, or science. They write software to handle specific jobs, such as a program used in an inventory control system or one to guide a missile after it has been fired. They also may work alone to revise existing packaged software. Systems programmers, on the other hand, maintain the software that controls the operation of an entire computer system. These workers make changes in the sets of instructions that determine how the central processing unit of the system handles the various jobs it has been given and communicates with peripheral equipment, such as terminals, printers, and disk drives. Because of their knowledge of the entire computer system, systems programmers often help applications programmers determine the source of problems that may occur with their programs.

Working Conditions

Computer scientists, systems analysts, and programmers often work in offices or laboratories in comfortable surroundings. They usually work about forty hours a week. Occasionally, however, evening or weekend work may become necessary so that they can meet their deadlines.

Because computer professionals spend long periods of time in front of a computer terminal typing on a keyboard, they are susceptible to eye strain and back discomfort as well as hand and wrist problems.

Training

Computer Scientists and Systems Analysts

There is no universally accepted way to prepare for a job as a computer professional because employers' preferences depend on the work being done. Prior work experience is very important. Many persons develop an area of expertise in their jobs, which tends to make them more marketable to employers. For example, people move into systems analyst jobs after working as computer programmers. Another example is the auditor in an accounting department who becomes a systems analyst specializing in accounting systems development.

College graduates almost always are sought for computer professional positions, and, for some of the more complex jobs, persons with graduate degrees are preferred. Generally, a computer scientist working in a research lab or academic institution will hold a doctorate or master's degree in computer science or engineering. Some computer scientists are able to gain sufficient experience for this type of position with only a bachelor's degree, but this is more difficult. Computer engineers generally have bachelor's degrees in computer engineering, electrical engineering, or math.

Employers usually want systems analysts to have a background in business management or a closely related field for work in a business environment, while a background in the physical sciences, applied mathematics, or engineering is preferred for work in science-oriented organizations. Many employers seek applicants who have bachelor's degrees in computer science, information science, computer information systems, or data processing.

Regardless of college major, employers look for people who are familiar with programming languages and have a broad knowledge of computer systems and technologies. Courses in computer programming or systems design offer good preparation for a job in this field.

Systems analysts must be able to think logically, have good communication skills, and like working with ideas and people. They often deal with a number of tasks simultaneously. The ability to concentrate and pay close attention to detail also is important.

Although systems analysts often work independently, they also work in teams on large projects. They must be able to communicate effectively with technical personnel, such as programmers and managers, as well as with other staff who have no technical computer background.

Technological advances come so rapidly in the computer field that continuous study is necessary to keep skills up-to-date. Continuing education is usually offered by employers, hardware and software vendors, colleges and universities, or private training institutions. Additional training may come from professional development seminars offered by professional computing societies.

Computer Programmers

Computer programming is taught at public and private vocational schools, community and junior colleges, and universities. High schools in many parts of the country also offer introductory courses in data processing. Many programmers obtain two-year degrees or certificates. Two-year colleges are targeted toward producing graduates for entry-level jobs and may have strong ties to the local job market.

The majority of programmers hold four-year degrees. Of these, some hold B.A. or B.S. degrees in computer science or information systems, while others have taken special courses in computer programming to supplement their study in fields such as accounting, inventory control, or other business areas. College graduates who are interested in changing careers or developing an area of expertise may return to a junior college for more training.

The level of education and quality of training that employers seek have been rising due to the growth in the number of qualified applicants and the increasing complexity of some programming tasks. Bachelor's degrees are now commonly required; in the absence of a degree, substantial specialized experience may be needed.

Employers using computers for scientific or engineering applications prefer college graduates who have degrees in computer or information science, mathematics, engineering, or the physical sciences. Graduate degrees are required for some jobs. Knowledge of C and FORTRAN programming languages is desirable since these are the most common languages used in this area.

Employers who use computers for business applications prefer to hire people who have had college courses in management information systems (MIS), programming, and business. Knowledge of COBOL, C, Fourth Generation Languages (4GL), CASE tools, C++, and other object-oriented programming languages is highly desirable.

Employers often prefer general business skills and experience related to the operations of the firm. In the future, it may be common for applications programmers to obtain a multidisciplinary degree to provide adequate knowledge of the particular application area along with programming skills. A relatively small number of employers promote workers such as computer operators who have taken courses in programming to programmer jobs because of their knowledge of and particular work experience with the firm's computer systems.

Most systems programmers hold four-year degrees in computer science. Extensive knowledge of operating systems is essential. This includes being able to configure the operating system to work with different types of hardware and adapting the operating system to best meet the needs of the particular company.

When hiring programmers, employers look for people who can think logically and who are capable of exacting analytical work. The job calls for patience, persistence, and the ability to work with extreme accuracy even under pressure. Ingenuity and imagination are also particularly important when programmers test their work for potential failures. Increasingly, interpersonal skills are valued because of the use of programmer teams and user support centers. The ability to work with abstract concepts and do technical analysis is especially important for systems programmers because they work with the software that controls the computer's operation.

Beginning programmers may spend their first weeks on the job attending training classes. After this initial instruction, they may work alone on simple assignments or on a team with more experienced programmers. Either way, they generally must spend at least several months working under close supervision. Because of rapidly changing technology, programmers must continuously update their training by taking courses sponsored by their employers or by software vendors.

Certification

The Institute for Certification of Computer Professionals offers the designation Certified Systems Professional (CSP) to those who have four years of experience and who pass a core examination plus exams in two specialty areas.

The Quality Assurance Institute awards the designation Certified Quality Analyst (CQA) to those who meet education and experience requirements, pass an exam, and endorse a code of ethics. Neither designation is mandatory, but either may provide a job seeker a competitive advantage.

Earnings

Median annual earnings of systems analysts who work full-time run about $42,100. The middle 50 percent earn between $32,000 and $52,200. The lowest 10 percent earn less than $25,200, and the highest 10 percent earn more than $65,500. Computer scientists with advanced degrees generally earn more than systems analysts.

In the federal government, the entrance salary for recent college graduates with bachelor's degrees is about $18,300 a year; for those with superior academic records, $22,700.

Median earnings of programmers who work full-time run about $35,600 a year. The lowest 10 percent earn less than $19,700, and the highest 10 percent, more than $58,000. On average, systems programmers earn more than applications programmers.

In the federal government, the entrance salary for programmers with college degrees or qualifying experience is about $18,300 a year; for those with a superior academic record, $22,700.

On-Line Opportunities

With the growth of computer on-line services such as America Online, Prodigy, and CompuServe, opportunities for employment have grown as well. Many of the services rely on volunteer help, offering a free account in exchange for on-line work, but paid positions also are available. One example is the America Online Campus, where thousands of students each month take a variety of courses from the comfort of their own homes, and instructors do their teaching from home as well.

On-line instructors usually have expertise in specific areas such as writing, math, or science, and offer courses on a part-time basis just as they would at a two- or four-year college or adult education facility.

Earnings for On-Line Instructors

Instructors are usually paid a set fee per student, starting at about $15 for a four-week course and going up to about $32.50 for a twelve-week course. So, obviously the amount of pay depends on the number of enrolled students.

What It's Really Like

Stephen Morrill, AOL On-Line Instructor

Stephen Morrill has been with America Online's Online Campus program since the fall of 1994. He teaches two courses: *Freelance Nonfiction Magazine Articles* and *Freelance Nonfiction Writing Business*. He also is a full-time freelance writer and the local correspondent in his home area for Reuters, the world's largest wire service. His stories are used by some 200,000 newspapers and TV and radio stations around the world.

WHAT AN ON-LINE JOB INVOLVES "The first course I teach, Freelance Nonfiction Magazine Articles, is intended to teach students how to write a research-based, standard nonfiction magazine article. I tell them how to do this, and guide them through a short sample article that they write, word by word.

"The other course, Freelance Nonfiction Writing Business, is intended to teach how to market yourself and how to run the business of nonfiction writing on a freelance basis. Nonfiction includes magazines, books, and assorted brochures and newsletters. The course touches upon all these but focuses most heavily upon the magazine market.

"There is a two-hour weekly session for eight weeks for both courses, during which we interact 'live' on-line. I upload additional material to a private library and students download that material, too.

"The classes consist of three parts. Each week I upload to our private library the materials they should read before the next class. In class we interact as much as the medium allows: we have questions and answers, and we do an in-class exercise or two. Each week students also receive an assignment to carry out.

"The job is really a lot of fun. I teach it for three reasons. First, I get cash for it. Second, I simply love to talk (or write) about freelancing, and I'm a good teacher, too. And third, it gets me pumped up for my own writing, sort of like going to weekend conferences but with pay.

"I put in a lot of hours off line, even with minimum critiquing of student manuscripts. I'm very determined to tell them all I know and to give them their money's worth. Students need a three-inch loose-leaf binder to hold the material from one course.

"I keep time down by automating things as much as possible. I can critique a fifteen hundred-word manuscript in about twenty minutes. This comes, frankly, from having seen almost every question or problem before and so having an answer ready at hand and also from just being a fast typist. And I am not ashamed to say 'I don't know' sometimes. I do usually try to suggest some other place to look for the answer.

"I get paid $27.50 per student here on AOL. It's a source of money; it's not a living. It probably averages about $10 per hour of work—slightly above the minimum wage and well below the $50 per hour that I shoot for in my writing. I also earn free AOL hours from teaching that give me the freedom to play on the Internet and the Web. I can use those extensively for researching my magazine and newspaper writing.

"On-line teaching permits me to shove a lot of material at the students, since they can download it and read it on their own. And the question/answer sessions are almost as good as the live ones. The biggest disadvantage to on-line teaching is the (current) inability to show students things. I cannot just hold up a *Writer's Market* and say, 'Buy this book,' or show them a sample of a spreadsheet printout or database printout (the spacing gets lost in the ascii transference so only the simplest layouts work). For off-line, in-person classes, I can bring boxes of magazines and books with me to use for illustration. But you can't do that on-line."

HOW STEPHEN MORRILL GOT STARTED   "I learned about the job on AOL through another AOL teacher who knew that I taught nonfiction writing at a local school and in seminars and that I had been a full-time freelancer for ten years. He asked me to come to

AOL and teach there. I first became a subscriber to the service, then sent a proposal and lesson plan to the Online Campus coordinator via E-mail. He let me try a freebie course first. Then I started teaching and getting paid."

TIPS FROM STEPHEN MORRILL   "Do it only if you already teach somewhere else or have some experience in teaching. Regard it as an adjunct to your real job; it's that other job that gives you the expertise to teach. Be extremely computer-literate and comfortable with, and knowledgeable about, the on-line Internet and Web worlds. Take a class or two on-line to see what it's all about before you jump in."

Finding On-Line Classes

To visit any on-line campus, you must already be a subscriber of the service. Check out the current course offerings and see where a course you'd like to teach might fit in. A little investigation will lead you to many opportunities.

CHAPTER SIX

Security Guards

Security guards, also called security officers, patrol and inspect property to protect against fire, theft, vandalism, and illegal entry. Their duties vary with the size, type, and location of the employer.

In office buildings, banks, hospitals, and department stores, guards protect records, merchandise, money, and equipment. In department stores, they often work with undercover detectives to watch for theft by customers or store employees.

At ports, airports, and railroads, guards protect merchandise being shipped as well as property and equipment. They screen passengers and visitors for weapons, explosives, and other contraband. They ensure that nothing is stolen while being loaded or unloaded, and they watch for fires, prowlers, and trouble among work crews. Sometimes they direct traffic.

Guards who work in museums or art galleries protect paintings and exhibits. They also answer routine questions from visitors and sometimes guide tours.

In factories, laboratories, government buildings, data processing centers, and military bases, where valuable property or information such as information on new products, computer codes, or defense secrets must be protected, guards check the credentials of persons and vehicles entering and leaving the premises. University, park, or recreation guards perform similar duties and also may issue parking permits and direct traffic. Golf course patrollers prevent unauthorized persons from using the facilities and help keep play running smoothly.

At social affairs, sports events, conventions, and other public gatherings, guards provide information, assist in crowd control, and watch for persons who may cause trouble. Some guards work as bouncers and patrol places of entertainment such as nightclubs to preserve order among customers and to protect property.

Armored car guards protect money and valuables during transit. Bodyguards protect individuals from bodily injury, kidnapping, or invasion of privacy.

In a large organization, a security officer often is in charge of the guard force; in a small organization, a single worker may be responsible for all security measures. Patrolling usually is done on foot, but if the property is large, guards may make their rounds by car or motor scooter.

As more businesses purchase advanced electronic security systems to protect their property, more guards are being assigned to stations from which they can monitor perimeter security, environmental functions, communications, and other systems. In many cases, these guards maintain radio contact with other guards patrolling on foot or in motor vehicles. Some guards use computers to store information on matters relevant to security, such as visitors or suspicious occurrences during their hours on duty.

As they make their rounds, guards check all doors and windows, see that no unauthorized persons remain after working hours, and ensure that fire extinguishers, alarms, sprinkler systems, furnaces, and various electrical and plumbing systems are working properly. They sometimes set thermostats or turn on lights for janitorial workers.

Guards usually are uniformed and may carry nightsticks and guns, although the bearing of guns is decreasing. They also may carry flashlights, whistles, two-way radios, and watch clock devices that indicate the time at which they reach various checkpoints.

Guards work indoors and outdoors patrolling buildings, industrial plants, and grounds. Indoors, they may be stationed at a guard desk to monitor electronic security and surveillance devices or to check the credentials of persons entering or leaving the premises. They also may be stationed at gate shelters or may patrol grounds in all weather.

Because guards often work alone, there may be no one nearby to help if an accident or injury occurs. Some large firms, therefore, use a reporting service that enables guards to be in constant contact with a central station outside the plant. If they fail to transmit an expected signal, the central station investigates.

Guard work is usually routine, but guards must be constantly alert for threats to themselves and to the property that they are protecting. Guards who work during the day may have a great deal of contact with other employees and members of the public.

Many guards work alone at night; the usual shift lasts eight hours. Some employers have three shifts, and guards rotate to divide daytime, weekend, and holiday work equally. Guards usually eat on the job instead of taking a regular break.

Guards held about 867,000 jobs in 1994. Industrial security firms and guard agencies employed 55 percent of all guards. These organizations provide security services on contract, assigning their guards to buildings and other sites as needed. The remainder were in-house guards, employed in large numbers by banks; building management companies; hotels; hospitals; retail stores; restaurants and bars; schools, colleges, and universities; and federal, state, and local governments. Although guard jobs are found throughout the country, most are located in metropolitan areas.

Training

Most employers prefer guards who are high school graduates. Applicants with less than a high school education also can qualify if they pass reading and writing tests and demonstrate competence in following written and oral instructions. Some jobs require a driver's license.

Employers also seek people who have had experience in the military police or in state and local police departments. Most persons who enter guard jobs have prior work experience, although it is usually unrelated. Because of limited formal training requirements and flexible hours, this occupation attracts some persons seeking a second job. For some, such as those who have retired from military careers or other protective services, guard employment is a second career.

Applicants are expected to have good character references, no police record, good health—especially in hearing and vision—and good personal habits such as neatness and dependability. They should be mentally alert, emotionally stable, and physically fit in order to cope with emergencies. Guards who have frequent contact with the public should be friendly and personable.

Some employers require applicants to take a polygraph examination or a written test of honesty, attitudes, and other personal qualities. Most employers require applicants and experienced workers to submit to drug screening tests as a condition of employment.

Virtually all states and the District of Columbia have licensing or registration requirements for guards who work for contract security agencies. Registration generally requires that employment of an individual as a guard be reported to the licensing authorities, the state police department, or other state licensing commission. To be granted a license as a guard, individuals generally must be eighteen years old, have no convictions for perjury or acts of violence, pass a background examination, and complete classroom training in such subjects as property rights, emergency procedures, and seizure of suspected criminals. In 1990, only about five states and the District of Columbia had licensing requirements for in-house guards.

Candidates for guard jobs in the federal government must have some experience as a guard and pass a written examination. Armed forces experience also is an asset. For most federal guard positions, applicants must qualify in the use of firearms.

The amount of training guards receive varies. Training requirements generally are increasing as modern, highly sophisticated security systems become more commonplace. Many employers give newly hired guards instruction before they start the job and also provide several weeks of on-the-job training. More and more states are making ongoing training a legal requirement. For example, New York State now requires guards to complete forty hours of training after starting work. Guards receive training in protection, public relations, report writing, crisis deterrence, first aid, and drug control, as well as specialized training relevant to particular assignments. Guards employed at establishments that place a heavy emphasis on security usually receive extensive formal training. For example, guards at nuclear power plants may undergo several months of training before being placed on duty under close supervision.

Guards may be taught to use firearms, administer first aid, operate alarm systems and electronic security equipment, and spot and deal with security problems. Guards who are authorized to carry firearms may be periodically tested in their use according to state or local laws. Some guards are periodically tested for strength and endurance.

Although guards in small companies receive periodic salary increases, advancement is likely to be limited. However, most large organizations use a military type of ranking that offers advancement in position and salary. Higher-level guard experience may enable persons to transfer to police jobs that offer better pay and greater opportunities for advancement. Guards with some college education may advance to jobs that involve administrative duties or the prevention of espionage and sabotage. A few guards with management skills open their own contract security guard agencies.

Job Outlook

Job openings for guards are expected to continue to be plentiful. High turnover and this occupation's large size rank it among those providing the greatest number of job openings in the entire economy. Many opportunities are expected for full-time employment as well as for those seeking part-time work or second jobs at night or on weekends. However, some competition is expected for the higher-paying in-house guard positions. Compared to contract security guards, in-house guards enjoy higher earnings and benefits, greater job security, and more advancement potential, and they are usually given more training and responsibility.

Employment of guards is expected to grow much faster than the average for all occupations through the year 2005. Increased concern about crime, vandalism, and terrorism will heighten the need for security in and around plants, stores, offices, and recreation areas. The level of business investment in increasingly expensive plants and equipment is expected to rise, resulting in growth in the number of guard jobs. Demand for guards will also grow as private security firms increasingly perform duties such as monitoring crowds at airports and providing security in courts formerly handled by government police officers and marshals.

Because engaging the services of a security guard firm is easier and less costly than assuming direct responsibility for hiring, training, and managing a security guard force, job growth is expected to be concentrated among contract security guard agencies.

Guards employed by industrial security and guard agencies occasionally are laid off when the firm at which they work does not renew its contract with the agency. Most are able to find employment with other agencies, however. Guards employed directly by the firm at which they work are seldom laid off because a plant or factory must still be protected even when economic conditions force it to close temporarily.

Salaries

According to a survey of workplaces in 160 metropolitan areas, guards with the least responsibility and training had median hourly earnings of $6.00 in 1993. Those in the middle half earned between $5.00 and $7.35 an hour. Guards who had more specialized training and experience had median hourly earnings of $11.20.

Unionized in-house guards tend to earn more than the average. Many guards are represented by the United Plant Guard Workers of America. Other guards belong to the International Guards Union of America or the International Union of Security Officers.

Depending on their experience, newly hired guards in the federal government earned between $14,900 and $16,700 a year in 1995. Beginning salaries were slightly higher in selected areas where the prevailing local pay level was higher. Overall, guards employed by the federal government averaged about $23,300 a year in 1995. These workers usually receive overtime pay as well as a wage differential for the second and third shifts.

What It's Really Like

Timothy T. Speed Jr., Security Supervisor
Timothy T. Speed Jr. is the security supervisor for a large apartment complex in Oklahoma City, Oklahoma. He has been in this field since 1994.

HOW TIMOTHY SPEED GOT STARTED   "I wanted to do something to help people, and what better way to help people than to make them feel safe in their own homes and office buildings.

"The first security job I got was through a friend I met at the local gun range. She was leaving a position with a security agency to start a job as a corrections officer. I applied and got the job, with my friend's recommendation, of course.

"In Oklahoma everyone must go through a training program before they can get anything other than a conditional license. I paid for all of my training. After I got my first security job and had my conditional security license, I received training for the Unarmed License at the Metro Vo-Tech School in Oklahoma City. This class is forty hours long. You have to have perfect attendance and pass all six tests with an 80 percent or better.

"I have also received training for certification with an ASP baton, an expandable night stick. In October of 1994 I received training for the Armed Security Officer License. The next month I was trained to carry a semiautomatic pistol. The next year I was trained for the 12-gauge pump shotgun.

"The Armed Security License Training consists of eight hours of class time and sixteen hours on the firearms range. The Automatic Pistol Training consisted of eight hours of range time with the same qualification as the revolver training."

ON THE JOB   "Most days are a bit on the boring side. There are many times when you do nothing more than sit, stand, or patrol your post and nothing happens. Then there are days you are so busy you wonder where the time went.

"The atmosphere is mostly quiet on one-officer posts. One-officer posts are those deemed by the powers that be to require only one officer to keep the post secure. These one-officer posts can be anything from warehouses to office buildings with secured entry points, meaning the officer stands or sits at a guard station. Some warehouses have day and night security. The day officer controls the entry point to make sure no unauthorized personnel enter the building, while the nighttime officer ensures the security of the premises by patrolling the interior and exterior for people who might try to break in.

"At most times during the week our apartment complex is a one-officer post, but during the weekend the post can have as many as three officers on duty.

"Securing an apartment community can be very stressful because we, as security officers, want to keep the peace for the tenants. We are responsible for handling loud noise complaints as well as domestic situations, and these types of calls seem to build, with everything being quiet for months at a time and then the tension breaks and everything goes wild.

"There are times that it can be very dangerous. Some people, who are not the most law abiding to begin with, think that we security officers don't have the right to tell them what to do. Some of them would just as soon kill you as look at you.

"But really, most of the people are nice. The downside to this work is that there is very little upward momentum, and the pay rate for an armed officer is around $5.50 an hour. With most security agencies I have worked for you are lucky to get minimum wage.

"Here on this job, though, if you work full-time, you get a salary and an apartment. Part-time officers work thirteen hours a week in exchange for an apartment. All officers are required to live on the property in case something big happens."

TIPS FROM TIMOTHY SPEED   "My advice to anyone entering this field is to use the experience as a stepping-stone to bigger and better things. A career as a police officer would be a good place to take this. In this field as a security officer you sometimes will be placed in situations that not even some police officers would want to find themselves, and this provides practical experience for any law enforcement position.

"Secondly, always treat the people you deal with the way you would want to be treated, but also keep them at a distance— because no human being is predictable. In essence, I am saying to treat every person as a possible threat.

"Lastly, if you can help it, never work an unarmed post because the firearm at your side is a great deterrent to would-be criminals. As a safety precaution I suggest you purchase a bulletproof vest and wear it at all times while on duty.

"Always be alert, even if it's been quiet for months, because this is when things start to happen. Always, no matter what the person you are dealing with calls you, keep a professional attitude and perspective on the job. If you let them get to you, you have most definitely lost the battle and let them win.

"And you should realize that most security positions are worked at night, forty hours a week, including weekends, so if you're in this field, be prepared to give up weekends because that is when our job is done."

CHAPTER SEVEN

Forest Rangers

F orests and rangelands serve a variety of needs: they supply wood products, livestock, forage, minerals, and water; serve as sites for recreational activities; and provide habitats for wildlife.

Although much of the work is solitary, foresters and conservation scientists also deal regularly with landowners, loggers, forestry technicians and aides, farmers, ranchers, government officials, special-interest groups, and the public in general.

While some professionals in this category work out of doors, others work in offices or labs. The outdoor work can be physically demanding. There's the weather to deal with, and some foresters may need to walk long distances through heavily wooded areas to carry out their work.

Foresters may also work long hours fighting forest fires, and conservation scientists are called into the field to prevent erosion after a forest fire. They may also provide emergency help after floods, mud slides, and tropical storms.

Job Titles in Forestry

There are several categories of workers that fall into this career area: foresters, range managers (also called range conservationists, range ecologists, or range scientists), conservation scientists, soil conservationists, forest rangers, park rangers, forestry technicians, and forest workers.

Foresters

Foresters manage forested land for a variety of purposes, working for private timber companies or for county, state, or federal government forestry departments.

Timber Management

Those working in private industry may procure timber from private landowners. To do this, foresters contact local forest owners and gain permission to take inventory of the type, amount, and location of all standing timber on the property, a process known as timber cruising. Foresters then appraise the timber's worth, negotiate terms for removing the timber, and draw up a contract for procurement. Next, they subcontract with loggers or pulpwood cutters for tree removal and aid in road layout. They also maintain close contact with the subcontractor's workers and the landowner to ensure that the work meets the landowner's requirements, as well as federal, state, and local environmental specifications. Forestry consultants often act as agents for the forest owner, performing the above duties and negotiating timber sales with industrial procurement foresters.

Throughout the process, foresters consider the economics of the purchase as well as the environmental impact on natural resources, a function that has taken on added importance in recent years. To do this, they determine how best to conserve wildlife habitats, creek beds, water quality, and soil stability and how best to comply with environmental regulations. Foresters must balance the desire to conserve forested ecosystems for future generations with the need to use forest resources for recreational and economic purposes.

Regeneration

Foresters also supervise the planting and growing of new trees, a process called regeneration. They choose and prepare the site, using controlled burning, bulldozers, or herbicides to clear weeds, brush, and logging debris. They advise on the type, number, and placement of trees to be planted. Foresters then monitor the trees to ensure healthy growth and to determine the best time for harvesting. If they detect signs of disease or harmful insects, they decide on the best course of treatment to prevent contamination or infestation of healthy trees.

Public Use Management

Foresters who work for the county, state, or federal government manage public forests and parks and also work with private landowners to protect and manage forestland outside of the public domain. They may also design recreation areas and campgrounds. See the information on the National Park Service later in this chapter.

Range Managers

Range managers—also called range conservationists, range ecologists, or range scientists—manage, improve, and protect rangelands to maximize their use without damaging the environment. Rangelands cover about one billion acres of the United States, mostly in the western states and Alaska. They contain many natural resources, including grass and shrubs for animal grazing, wildlife habitats, water from vast watersheds, recreation facilities, and valuable mineral and energy resources.

Range managers also help ranchers attain optimum livestock production by determining the number and kind of animals to graze, the grazing system to use, and the best season for grazing. At the same time, however, they must maintain soil stability and vegetation for other uses such as wildlife habitats and outdoor recreation. They also plan and implement revegetation of disturbed sites.

Soil Conservationists

Soil conservationists provide technical assistant to farmers, ranchers, state and local governments, and others concerned with the conservation of soil, water, and related natural resources. They develop programs designed to get the most productive use of land without damaging it.

Conservationists visit areas with erosion problems, find the source of the problem, and help landowners and managers develop management practices to combat it. Conservation scientists and foresters often specialize in one area, such as forest resource management, urban forestry, wood technology, or forest economics.

What It's Really Like

Dr. Ronald Miller, Independent Consultant

Dr. Ronald Miller is a specialist in biodiversity conservation planning. He works for Pioneer Geographic Designs in Northampton, Massachusetts, a firm involved in providing environmental planning assistance at the international, national, regional, and local levels. The company specializes in the use of computerized information technologies, including the design and creation of maps and databases.

Dr. Miller has an impressive list of educational credentials: his B.A. from the department of environmental sciences at Brandeis University in Waltham, Massachusetts; his M.S. from the department of forestry and wildlife ecology at the University of Florida in Gainesville; further graduate study in the department of biological sciences at Harvard University; and his Ph.D. from the Institute of Ecology at the University of Georgia in Athens, which he earned in 1985. He has been working steadily in the field since.

ON THE JOB   "Field science interested me at an early age. I have always wanted to work with and for the protection of plants and animals. I edited two scientific journals at the Museum of Comparative Zoology at Harvard University for two and a half years.

"Now, working as a consultant, I get to focus upon many different categories of biological conservation and on many different regions of the world. I must often work long hours to prepare long and meticulous reports. However, I get to work very independently and I usually get to conduct the work in the ways that I see as most effective.

"The most enjoyable part of the work is being able to travel to many different regions. For example, I recently gave a presentation of my work at the annual meeting of the International Union of Forestry Research Organizations in Tampere, Finland.

"The most difficult part of being a consultant is having to go through sometimes long periods without income. For example, I have gone through almost one year without a paid position. Also, I must provide myself with health insurance and retirement, both of which are expensive."

SOME TIPS FROM DR. MILLER   "If possible, you should identify what you are most interested in while you are in college. Then, you should apply for any significant opportunities that you become aware of that will allow you to gain experience in this field. Don't think that any opportunities that you see advertised are too good for someone like yourself—go for it."

Training Paths

Summer jobs may not require specific training, but if you're interested in a career, you'll want to consider a college degree.

Forestry

A bachelor's degree is usually the minimum requirement for any professional career in forestry. In the federal government, a combination of experience and appropriate education may occasionally substitute for a four-year degree, but the stiff job competition makes this difficult.

Fourteen states have either mandatory licensing or voluntary registration requirements a forester must meet to acquire the title Professional Forester. Becoming licensed or registered usually requires a four-year degree in forestry, a minimum period of training time, and passing an exam.

Foresters who wish to perform specialized research or teach should have an advanced degree, preferably a Ph.D.

About sixty colleges and universities offer bachelor's or higher degrees in forestry; more than forty are accredited by the Society of American Foresters. The various college programs stress science, mathematics, communications skills, and computer science, as well as technical forestry subjects. Courses in forest economics and business administration are recommended to supplement scientific and technical knowledge.

Prospective foresters must have a strong grasp of policy issues and of the increasingly numerous and complex environmental regulations that affect many forestry-related activities. Many colleges require students to complete a field session either in a camp operated by the college or in a cooperative work-study program with a federal or state agency or in private industry. All schools encourage students to take summer jobs that provide experience in forestry or conservation work.

Range Management

A bachelor's degree is also the minimum requirement for any professional career in range management or range science, and graduate degrees are required for teaching and research positions.

Approximately thirty-one schools offer degree programs in range management or range science or in closely related disciplines with a range science or range management option.

Specialized range management courses combine plant, animal, and soil sciences with principles of ecology and resource management. Electives usually include economics, forestry, hydrology, agronomy, wildlife, animal husbandry, computer science, and recreation.

Soil Conservation

Very few schools offer degrees in soil conservation. Most soil conservationists have degrees in environmental studies, agronomy, general agriculture, hydrology, or crop or soil science; a few have degrees in related fields such as wildlife biology, forestry, or range management.

The Soil and Water Conservation Society sponsors a certification program based on education, experience, and testing. Completing the program allows you the designation of Certified Professional Erosion and Sediment Control Specialist. The Soil and Water Conservation Society's address is in the Appendix.

The Job Outlook

The job outlook in forestry professions is good. Demands for professionals will be spurred by a continuing emphasis on environmental protection and responsible land management. For example, urban foresters are increasingly needed to do environmental impact studies in urban areas and to help regional planning commissions to make land-use decisions, particularly in the northeast and in other major population centers of the country.

Nationally, the Stewardship Incentive Program, funded by the federal government, provides money to the states to encourage landowners to practice multiple-use forest management. As a result, foresters are needed to assist landowners in making decisions about how to manage their forested property.

Job opportunities for soil conservationists will also grow because government regulations, such as those regarding the management of storm water and coastlines, have created demand for experts knowledgeable about erosion, not only on farms, but in cities and suburbs.

In private industry, more foresters should be needed to improve forest and logging practices, increase output and profitability, and deal with environmental regulations.

Budgetary constraints may affect opportunities in the federal government. Also, federal land management agencies, such as the U.S. Forest Service, are de-emphasizing timber programs and focusing increasingly on wildlife, recreation, and sustaining ecosystems. This increases the demand for other life and social scientists related to foresters.

Certain areas of the country offer more job opportunities for foresters and range conservationists than others. Most employment is concentrated in the West and Midwest, and most forestry-related employment is in the South and West.

Salaries

Most graduates entering the federal government with bachelor's degrees in forestry, range management, or soil conservation start at about $19,000 to $24,000 a year, depending upon academic achievement. Master's degree holders start from $24,000 to $28,000, and Ph.D. holders start at $35,000 or, in research positions, at $42,000.

Beginning salaries can run slightly higher in areas where the prevailing local pay is higher. In 1995 the average salary for federal foresters in nonsupervisory, supervisory, and managerial positions was $44,700; for soil conservationists, $42,220; and for forest product technologists, $58,680.

In private industry, starting salaries for bachelor's degree graduates are comparable to starting salaries in the federal government, but starting salaries in state and local government are generally lower.

Foresters and conservation scientists working for the government or in large private firms generally receive more generous benefits, such as pension plans, health and life insurance, and paid vacations, than those working for smaller firms.

Related Jobs in the National Park Service

The National Park Service, a bureau under the U.S. Department of the Interior (not to confused with the U.S. Forest Service under the U.S. Department of Agriculture) encompasses more than 350 historic, natural, and recreational areas across the country, including the Grand Canyon, Yellowstone National Park, and Lake Mead. The National Park Service provides a variety of opportunities for people interested in working on their own in the great outdoors.

Because most sites are not located near major cities, serious candidates must, for the most part, be prepared to relocate. Housing may or may not be provided, depending upon the site and your position.

Park Rangers

To protect resources and to serve the public, the National Park Service employs both a permanent and seasonal workforce. Park rangers are hired into one of three categories, though job duties often overlap.

Law Enforcement

Park rangers in the law enforcement category patrol park roads and visitor areas, providing for visitor safety. They also may provide interpretive and other information as well as respond to emergency situations.

Interpretation

Duties vary greatly from position to position and site to site, but rangers in the interpretation division are usually responsible for developing and presenting programs that explain a park's historic, cultural, or archeological features. This is done through talks, demonstrations, and guided walking tours. Rangers also sit at information desks, provide visitor services, or participate in conservation or restoration projects. Entry-level employees might also collect fees, provide first aid, and operate audiovisual equipment.

General Duty

Individuals interested in and qualified for forestry and related fields would be placed in this category with the National Park Service. General-duty park rangers perform a variety of services, including fee collection and law enforcement. Those with appropriate backgrounds work with backcountry, campground, recreation, or forestry or resource management.

Other responsibilities within parks or conservation areas might include conservation and restoration activities, fire control, wildlife management, and insect or plant disease control.

Qualifications and Salaries with the National Park Service

In determining a candidate's eligibility for employment, and at which salary level he or she would be placed, the National Park Service weighs several factors. In essence, those with the least experience or education will begin at the lowest federal government salary grade of GS-2. But the requirements for that grade are only six months of experience in related work or a high school diploma or its equivalency.

The more related work experience or education, the higher the salary level. For example, GS-4 requires eighteen months of general experience in park operations or in related fields and six months of specialized experience or one ninety-day season as a seasonal park ranger at the GS-3 level.

Completion of two academic years of college may be substituted for experience if the course work covers social science, history, archeology, parks and recreation management, or other related disciplines.

Getting Your Foot in the Door

Competition for jobs, especially at the most well-known sites, can be fierce, but the National Park Service employs a huge permanent staff, and this is supplemented tenfold by an essential seasonal workforce during peak visitation periods.

The best way for a newcomer to break in is to start off with seasonal employment during school breaks. With a couple of summer seasons under your belt, the doors will open more easily for permanent employment.

And, because of Office of Personnel Management regulations, veterans of the U.S. Armed Forces have a decided advantage. Depending upon their experience, they may be given preference among applicants.

How to Apply

Recruitment for summer employment begins every year on September 1, with a January 15 deadline. Some sites, such as Death Valley or Everglades National Park, also have a busy winter season. The winter recruitment period is June 1 through July 15.

Applications for seasonal employment with the National Park Service can be obtained through the Office of Personnel Management or from:

U.S. Department of the Interior
National Park Service
Seasonal Employment Unit
P.O. Box 37127
Washington, DC 20013-7127

You may also contact directly the area in which you would like to work to request application forms and information on procedures. For a list of all concessions, contact any of the ten regional offices of the National Park Service. These addresses are listed in the Appendix.

Mail Carriers

E ach day, the U.S. Postal Service receives, sorts, and delivers millions of letters, bills, advertisements, and packages. To do this, it employs about 792,000 workers. Almost half of these workers are postal clerks, who sort mail and serve customers in post offices, or mail carriers, who deliver the mail.

Clerks and carriers are distinguished by the type of work they do. Clerks are usually classified by the mail processing function they perform, whereas carriers are classified by their type of route, city or rural.

Postal Clerks

About 350 mail processing centers throughout the country service post offices in surrounding areas and are staffed primarily by postal clerks. Some clerks, more commonly referred to as mail handlers, unload the sacks of incoming mail; separate letters, parcel post, magazines, and newspapers; and transport these to the proper sorting and processing areas. In addition, they may load mail into automated letter-sorting machines, perform simple canceling operations, and rewrap packages damaged in processing.

After letters have been put through stamp-canceling machines, they are taken to other workrooms to be sorted according to destination. Clerks operating older electronic letter-sorting machines push keys corresponding to the zip code of the local post office to which each letter will be delivered; the machine then drops the letters into the proper slots. This older, less automated method of letter sorting is being slowly phased out.

Other clerks sort odd-sized letters, magazines, and newspapers by hand. Finally, the mail is sent to local post offices for sorting according to delivery route before it is delivered by the mail carriers.

A growing proportion of clerks operate optical character readers (OCRs) and bar code sorters. Optical character readers read the zip code and spray a bar code onto the mail. Bar code sorters then scan the code and sort the mail. Because this is significantly faster than older sorting methods, it is becoming the standard sorting technology in mail processing centers.

Postal clerks at local post offices sort local mail for delivery to individual customers; sell stamps, money orders, postal stationary, and mailing envelopes and boxes; weigh packages to determine postage; and check that packages are in satisfactory condition for mailing. Clerks also register, certify, and insure mail and answer questions about postage rates, post office boxes, mailing restrictions, and other postal matters. Occasionally, they may help a customer file a claim for a damaged package.

Mail Carriers

Once the mail has been processed and sorted, it is ready to be delivered by mail carriers. Duties of city and rural carriers are very similar. Most travel established routes delivering and collecting mail. Mail carriers start work at the post office early in the morning, where they spend a few hours arranging their mail for delivery. Recently, automated equipment has been able to sort most of the mail for city carriers, allowing them to spend less time sorting and more time delivering mail.

Carriers may cover their routes on foot, by vehicle, or a combination of both. On foot, they carry a heavy load of mail in a satchel or push it in a cart. In some urban and most rural areas, they use a car or small truck. Although the Postal Service provides vehicles to city carriers, most rural carriers use their own automobiles. Deliveries are made house-to-house, to roadside mailboxes, and to large buildings, such as offices or apartments, which generally have all the mailboxes on the first floor.

Besides delivering and collecting mail, carriers collect money for postage due and COD (cash on delivery) fees and obtain signed receipts for registered, certified, and insured mail. If a customer is not home, the carrier leaves a notice that tells where special mail is being held.

After completing their routes, carriers return to the post office with mail gathered from street collection boxes, homes, and businesses. They turn in the mail receipts and money collected during the day and may separate letters and parcels for further processing by clerks.

The duties of some city carriers may be very specialized; some deliver only parcel post while others collect mail from street boxes and receiving boxes in office buildings. In contrast, rural carriers provide a wide range of postal services. In addition to delivering and picking up mail, they sell stamps and money orders and accept parcels, letters, and items to be registered, certified, or insured.

All carriers answer customer questions about postal regulations and services and provide change-of-address cards and other postal forms when requested. In addition to their regularly scheduled duties, carriers often participate in neighborhood service programs in which they check on elderly or shut-in patrons or notify the police of any suspicious activities along their routes.

Training

Postal clerks and mail carriers must be U.S. citizens or have been granted permanent resident-alien status in the United States. They must be at least eighteen years old (or sixteen, if they have a high school diploma). Qualification is based on a written examination that measures speed and accuracy at checking names and numbers and the ability to memorize mail distribution procedures. Applicants must pass a physical examination as well and may be asked to show that they can lift and handle mail sacks weighing up to seventy pounds.

Applicants for jobs as postal clerks operating electronic sorting machines must pass a special examination that includes a machine aptitude test. Applicants for mail carrier positions must have a driver's license and a good driving record and must achieve a passing grade on a road test.

Applicants should apply at the post office or mail processing center where they wish to work in order to determine when an exam will be given. Applicants' names are listed in order of their examination scores. Five points are added to the score of an honorably discharged veteran, and ten points to the score of a veteran wounded in combat or disabled.

When a vacancy occurs, the appointing officer chooses one of the top three applicants; the rest of the names remain on the list to be considered for future openings until their eligibility expires, usually two years from the examination date.

Relatively few people under the age of twenty-five are hired as career postal clerks or mail carriers, a result of keen competition for these jobs and the customary waiting period of one to two years or more after passing the examination. It is not surprising, therefore, that most entrants transfer from other occupations.

New postal clerks and mail carriers are trained on the job by experienced workers. Many post offices offer classroom instruction. Workers receive additional instruction when new equipment or procedures are introduced. They usually are trained by another postal employee or, sometimes, a training specialist hired under contract by the Postal Service.

Job Outlook

Those seeking a job in the Postal Service can expect to encounter keen competition. The number of applicants for postal clerk and mail carrier positions is expected to continue to far exceed the number of openings. Job opportunities will vary by occupation and duties performed.

Overall employment of postal clerks is expected to decline through the year 2005. In spite of anticipated increases in the total volume of mail, automation will continue to increase the productivity of postal clerks, slowing employment growth. Increasingly, mail will be moved using automated materials-handling equipment and sorted using optical character readers, bar code sorters, and other automated sorting equipment. In addition, demand for window clerks will be moderated by the increased sales of stamps and other postal products by grocery and department stores and other retail outlets.

Jobs will become available because of the need to replace postal clerks and mail carriers who retire or stop working for other reasons. However, the factors that make entry to these occupations—highly competitive attractive salaries, a good pension plan, job security, and modest educational requirements—contribute to a high degree of job attachment. Accordingly, replacement needs produce relatively fewer job openings than in other occupations of this size. In contrast to the typical pattern, postal workers generally remain in their jobs until they retire; relatively few transfer to other occupations.

Although the volume of mail to be processed and delivered rises and falls with the level of business activity, as well as with the season of the year, full-time postal clerks and mail carriers have never been laid off. When mail volume is high, full-time clerks and carriers work overtime, part-time clerks and carriers work additional hours, and casual clerks and carriers may be hired. When mail volume is low, overtime is curtailed, part-timers work fewer hours, and casual workers are discharged.

Salaries for Postal Workers

In 1995, base pay for beginning full-time carriers and postal clerks was $25,240 a year, rising to a maximum of $35,604 after twelve and a half years of service. For those working between 6 P.M. and 6 A.M., a supplement is paid. Experienced, full-time, city delivery mail carriers earn an average salary of $34,566 a year.

Postal clerks and carriers working part-time flexible schedules begin at $12.59 an hour and, based on the number of years of service, increase to a maximum of $17.76 an hour.

Rural delivery carriers had average base salaries of $33,980 in 1995. Their earnings are determined through an evaluation of the amount of work required to service their routes. Carriers with heavier workloads generally earn more than those with lighter workloads. Rural carriers also receive an equipment maintenance allowance when required to use their own vehicles. In 1995, this was approximately thirty-five cents per mile.

Postal workers enjoy a variety of employer-provided benefits. These include health and life insurance, vacation and sick leave, and a pension plan.

In addition to the hourly wage and benefits package, some postal workers receive a uniform allowance. This group includes various maintenance workers and those workers who are in the public view for four or more hours each day. The amount of the allowance depends on the job performed. Some workers are only required to wear a partial uniform, and their allowance is lower. In 1995, for example, the allowance for a letter carrier was $252 per year, compared to $108 for a window clerk and $50 for a mail handler.

Most postal workers belong to one of four unions: American Postal Workers Union, National Association of Letter Carriers, National Postal Mail Handlers Union, and National Rural Letter Carriers Association.

Related Fields

Others with duties related to those of mail carriers include messengers, merchandise deliverers, and delivery-route truck drivers.

Employers include major parcel delivery companies such as United Parcel Service and Federal Express as well as local, regional, and national delivery companies. Most major cities have interoffice delivery companies that employ bicycle riders to deliver packages within the downtown area.

What It's Really Like

Nick Delia, Letter Carrier

Nick Delia and his wife are both letter carriers. Nick has been working for the Postal Service for more than twelve years.

ON THE JOB   "You have to rely on your memory a lot in this job. You get to know who is living at a certain address, who's a forward. Forwarding the mail is the responsibility of the letter carrier.

"The majority of my route is a business route, which means I'm constantly in and out of the truck. For example, the local newspaper is on my route. I pull up to the building, take out their buckets of mail, take them into the mailroom, then get back into the truck and go to the next stop.

"I start at six o'clock in the morning. When I get in, most of the mail is already there. There are other clerks who get in at three or four in the morning. We first have to count our mail. It's counted by the foot. A certain number of letters makes up a foot. They come in trays, and there's two feet of mail, the letter size, stacked on a tray. Then you've got your magazines and newspapers. You need to know how many feet you have. That's how the amount of time you need to deliver the mail is calculated. In my particular case, fifteen feet of mail equals an eight-hour day. Anything over that, I'd need some overtime hours or some help.

"Then you have to go through all your mail, piece by piece, to check for forwards or holds. After that you have to put the mail into this large case we have, with all sorts of separations. You check the name and the address, then put it into the correct slot. When all your mail is up, you receive your accountable mail, your certified and registered letters. These you have to write up because they have to be signed for by the customer. Then you have your mark-up mail. That's the 'moved, left no forwarding address' or 'attempted, addressee unknown,' that sort of thing. Then you pull all the mail out of the case, and it comes out in the order you'll deliver it. After that, you bundle it up in rubber bands, then you pull out your parcels. Everything then goes out to your truck.

"This all takes about four hours. That's before you get out to the street. I'm usually out on the street by 10 A.M. It looks like the easiest job in the world, but most people have no idea what goes on behind the scenes. The delivery part is the easiest part of the day.

"But, of course, you have a lot to deal with on the street. That old saying, 'neither snow, nor sleet,' and all that is really true. It doesn't matter what the weather is, the mail has to go.

"We get the opportunity to put in a lot of overtime if we want, maybe even an extra $10,000 a year, and the base top pay for a letter carrier here is pretty good, about $35,400. But we earn our money. Not in every job do you have a dog chasing you down the street or find yourself working through a lightning storm. And we have traffic to deal with, too, and kids running out in the street. We've got our hazards.

"But basically, I think it's a good job. I get a feeling of accomplishment on my job. At the beginning of the day there's mail everywhere, but by the end of the day, there's nothing left, it's done. And I enjoy working outside, which is half of the job. I couldn't be a clerk, working indoors all day."

How Nick Delia Got Started   "I had some family members who were already in the post office. My last job, working for U-Haul, was going nowhere. The post office was giving the test, so I said, 'Let's try it.' It was basically a memory test, which has a lot to do with the job. I was called and started about twelve years ago."

SOME TIPS FROM NICK DELIA   "You've got to be physically fit. In addition, this is basically an unskilled job. Of course, you need a good memory and have to be intelligent, but if a person is not inclined to go to college, then this would be a good job."

APPENDIX

Professional Associations

F or more information on the careers covered in this book, contact the appropriate professional associations or related resource listed below.

Writers

Information about careers in writing can be obtained from:

American Society of Journalists and Authors
1501 Broadway
New York, NY 10036

Society of American Travel Writers
1155 Connecticut Avenue, Suite 500
Washington, DC 20006

For information on college internships in magazine editing, contact:

American Society of Magazine Editors
575 Lexington Avenue
New York, NY 10022

For information on careers in technical writing, contact:

Society for Technical Communication, Inc.
901 North Stuart Street, Suite 304
Arlington, VA 22203

Career information—including pamphlets titled "Facts About Newspapers" and "Newspaper: What's in It for Me?"—are available from:

Newspaper Association of America
The Newspaper Center
Box 17407
Dulles International Airport
Washington, DC 20041

Newspaper Association of America Foundation
11600 Sunrise Valley Drive
Reston, VA 22091

Information on careers in journalism, colleges and universities that offer degree programs in journalism or communications, and journalism scholarships and internships may be obtained from:

The Dow Jones Newspaper Fund, Inc.
P.O. Box 300
Princeton, NJ 08543-0300

For a list of junior and community colleges offering programs in journalism, contact:

Community College Journalism Association
San Antonio College
1300 San Pedro Avenue
San Antonio, TX 78212-4299

Information on union wage rates for newspaper and magazine reporters is available from:

The Newspaper Guild
Research and Information Department
8611 Second Avenue
Silver Spring, MD 20910

For a list of schools with accredited programs in journalism, send a stamped, self-addressed envelope to:

Accrediting Council on Education in Journalism and Mass Communication
University of Kansas School of Journalism
Stauffer-Flint Hall
Lawrence, KS 66045

For general information about careers in journalism, contact:

Association for Education in Journalism and Mass Communication
University of South Carolina
1621 College Street
Columbia, SC 29208-0251

A pamphlet titled "A Career in Newspapers" can be obtained from:

National Newspaper Association
1627 K Street NW, Suite 400
Washington, DC 20006

Names and locations of newspapers and a list of schools and departments of journalism are published in the annual *Editor and Publisher International Yearbook,* available in most public libraries and newspaper offices.

Artists

For information on careers in the visual arts, contact:

American Arts Alliance
1319 F Street NW, Suite 500
Washington, DC 20004

American Craft Council
Information Center
72 Spring Street
New York, NY 10012

American Society of Interior Designers
608 Massachusetts Avenue NE
Washington, DC 20002-6006

Association for Living Historical Farms and Agricultural
Museums
National Museum of American History
Room 5035
Smithsonian Institution
Washington, DC 20560

Costume Society of America
55 Edgewater Drive
P.O. Box 73
Earleville, MD 21919

The National Association of Schools of Art and Design
11250 Roger Bacon Drive, Suite 21
Reston, VA 22090-5202

National Assembly of Local Arts Agencies
927 Fifteenth Street NW, Twelfth Floor
Washington, DC 20005

National Assembly of State Arts Agencies
1010 Vermont Avenue NW, Suite 920
Washington, DC 20005

For information on careers in graphic design, contact:

The American Institute of Graphic Arts
1059 Third Avenue
New York, NY 10021-7602

For information on art careers in the publishing industry,
contact:

The Society of Publication Designers
60 East 42nd Street, Suite 721
New York, NY 10165-1416

Students in high school or college who are interested in careers
as illustrators should contact:

The National Association of Schools of Art and Design
11250 Roger Bacon Drive, Suite 21
Reston, VA 22090-5202

The Society of Illustrators
128 East 63rd Street
New York, NY 10021-7392

For information on careers in medical illustration, contact:

The Association of Medical Illustrators
1819 Peachtree Street NE, Suite 560
Atlanta, GA 30309-1848

For information on careers in scientific illustration, contact:

Guild of Natural Science Illustrators
P.O. Box 652, Ben Franklin Station
Washington, DC 20044-0652

Freelance Researchers

Accreditation Program
Family History Library
35 North West Temple Street
Salt Lake City, UT 84150

Board for Certification of Genealogists
P.O. Box 5816
Falmouth, VA 22403-5816

Computer Professionals

Further information about computer careers is available from:

Association for Computing Machinery
1515 Broadway
New York, NY 10036

Information about certification as a computer professional is available from:

Institute for the Certification of Computer Professionals
2200 East Devon Avenue, Suite 268
Des Plaines, IL 60018

Information about certification as a Certified Quality Analyst is available from:

Quality Assurance Institute
7575 Dr. Phillips Boulevard, Suite 350
Orlando, FL 32819

State employment service offices can provide information about job openings for computer programmers. Also check with your city's chamber of commerce for information on the area's largest employers.

Security Guards

Further information about work opportunities for guards is available from local employers and state employment service offices. Information about registration and licensing requirements for guards may be obtained from the state licensing commission or the state police department. In states where local jurisdictions establish licensing requirements, contact a local government authority such as the sheriff, county executive, or city manager.

Forest Rangers

For information about forestry careers or a list of forestry schools, send a self-addressed, stamped business envelope to:

Society of American Foresters
5400 Grosvenor Lane
Bethesda, MD 20814

For information about government forestry careers, contact:

Chief, U.S. Forest Service
U.S. Department of Agriculture
P.O. Box 96090
Washington, DC 20090-6090

For information about career in range management as well as a list of schools offering training, contact:

Society for Range Management
1839 York Street
Denver, CO 80206

For information about a career in soil conservation, contact:

Soil and Water Conservation Society
7515 Northeast Ankeny Road, RR #1
Ankeny, IA 50021-9764

For information about work as a park ranger, contact the nearest regional office of the National Park Service:

Alaska Region
National Park Service
2525 Gambell Street
Anchorage, AK 99503

Mid-Atlantic Region
National Park Service
143 South Third Street
Philadelphia, PA 19106

Midwest Region
National Park Service
1709 Jackson Street
Omaha, NE 68102

National Capital Region
National Park Service
1100 Ohio Drive SW
Washington, DC 20242

North Atlantic Region
National Park Service
15 State Street
Boston, MA 02109

Pacific Northwest Region
National Park Service
83 South King Street, #212
Seattle, WA 98104

Rocky Mountain Region
National Park Service
P.O. Box 25287
Denver, CO 80225

Southeast Region
National Park Service
Richard B. Russell Federal Building
75 Spring Street SW
Atlanta, GA 30303

Southwest Region
National Park Service
P.O. Box 728
Santa, Fe, NM 87501

Western Region
National Park Service
600 Harrison Street #600
San Francisco, CA 94107

Mail Carriers

Local post offices and state employment service offices can supply
details about entrance examinations and specific employment
opportunities for postal clerks and mail carriers.